Dan Colwell

contents

This Way Brazil   3

Flashback   6

The Southeast   13

   Rio de Janeiro 13, São Paulo 22,
   Espírito Santo 27, Minas Gerais 29

The South   35

   Paraná 35, Santa Catarina 39,
   Rio Grande do Sul 41

The Midwest   43

   Brasília 43, Mato Grosso
   and Mato Grosso do Sul 50

The Northeast   53

   Bahia 53, Pernambuco 59
   Rio Grande do Norte 63,
   Ceará 64, Maranhão 67

The North   68

   Amazonia 68

Cultural Notes   76

Shopping   78

Dining Out   80

Sports   84

The Hard Facts   86

Index   96

maps

Brasilia 93, Salvador 94,
São Luis 95

Fold-out maps

   Brazil,
   Rio de Janeiro, São Paulo

This Way Brazil

The Brazilians

One thing will remain constant as you travel throughout Brazil—its fascinating people. Here, the dream of society as a melting-pot has become reality, and the result is often dazzling.

A heady mixture of Indian, Portuguese and African elements has forged the Brazilian nation over a period of five centuries. The results are plain for all to see. Apart from the distinctive beauty of its people, those things which are now considered to be typically Brazilian—Carnival, samba music, the candomblé religion, and even the artistry of the national football team—are all evidence of the successful union of races and cultures to make one, remarkable nation.

A Big Country

The sheer scale of Brazil's geography takes the breath away. Larger than mainland United States, and more than twice the size of India, it is almost a continent in itself. Curiously, the distance between its furthest points east and west, 4,319 km (2,684 miles), is almost exactly the same as from north to south, 4,394 km (2,731 miles). That's the equivalent of going from London to Moscow. Brazil stretches over four time zones, borders on every country in South America except two, and has an Atlantic coastline measuring some 7,000 km (4,000 miles). Taking up approximately half the landmass of South America, it is the fifth-largest country in the world. But the majority of the population lives within 500 km (300 miles) of the coast.

Brazil's landscape is dominated by two all-important topographical features: the Amazon, the largest river in the world, containing 20 per cent of its fresh water; and the vast Central Highlands, a plateau 460 m (about 1,500 ft) above sea level, where many peaks tower at more than 2,600 m (8,000 ft). In what is known as the Great Escarpment, the Highlands plunge dramatically into the sea all the way along the Brazilian coastline from Porto Alegre in the south to Salvador in the northeast. This provides the stunning backdrop to Brazil's coastal cities such as Rio de Janeiro and Vitória.

Land of the Future

Many are surprised to find that Brazil can hold its own with the economic giants, too. It has a staggering wealth of natural resources: enormous deposits of gold, iron, manganese, bauxite and uranium. It turns out 90 per cent of the world's gemstones, has vast hardwood forests and is the world's largest supplier of sugar and coffee, as well as being one of the leading producers of rice, tobacco, cocoa, beef, cotton and several other goods.

Perhaps even more surprising, Brazil has sizeable modern oil, car manufacturing, electronics and aircraft industries, and its Itaipú dam is the largest hydro-electric plant in the world.

The US president who said that wherever Brazil goes the rest of the hemisphere must follow may have been flattering his southern neighbour. But as Brazil already is the tenth-largest economy in the world and promises an almost limitless potential, this bold statement may one day become fact.

Beleaguered Forest

When the world's leaders flocked to Rio in 1992 for the Earth Summit, the protection of the Amazon rainforest was uppermost in their minds. Concern about its steady destruction has captured global attention. Little wonder. The Amazon is the earth's lungs, producing a third of all our oxygen. It's also the biggest, most diverse botanical garden on the planet. Walk through a single acre of its 2.4 million sq km (1.5 million sq miles) and you will find more than 170 different species of tree (as opposed to 6 per acre in ordinary forests). Beneath its lush, green canopy, so thick in places that it puts the jungle into permanent night, lives the richest gene pool of plants and insects in the world. Incredibly, this amounts to perhaps 30 per cent of all the species in existence, with untold possibilities for pharmaceuticals and medicines.

One hope for the Amazon's future lies with tourism. Ultimately, people's interest in visiting the forest may prove more lucrative than chopping it down. Hence a trip to the Amazon not only offers the chance to marvel at this unique wonder first-hand, but also to contribute to its survival.

Festival Time

Brazilians have always put their own exuberant stamp on Catholic festivals. The most famous of all, known the world over, is *Carnaval*. Its origins lie in pagan celebrations of the rites of spring. Unable to suppress these festivities, the Catholic Church appropriated them instead, and they reappeared as a Christian festival, the last feast before the 40 days' abstinence of Lent. Some have suggested that the word derives from the phrase *carne vale*— "goodbye to meat". But despite the Church's hope that this would give the festivities a more spiritual cast, they never lost their saturnalian wildness. Indeed, when Carnival was first brought to Brazil by the Portuguese, its liveliness was only further enhanced by the presence of African slaves, whose masters allowed them to let off steam.

In its early days, Carnival was dominated by a wild pranksterism called *entrudo*. This involved the liberal use of stink bombs, water balloons, clouds of flour and even arson to annoy as many people as possible. It became so anarchic that many people preferred to stay indoors for the duration. Thankfully, *entrudo* was formally abolished in the 19th century.

Since then, Carnival has become essentially a fabulous costume ball, danced in the streets for five days and nights—and sometimes longer—by ordinary Brazilians. Rio de Janeiro's version has gained a world-wide reputation, but Carnival takes place with equal fervour in cities all over Brazil. An explosion of colour and joy, a riot of dancing, outrageous costumes, pulsating samba and sheer sexiness, it encapsulates the very essence of the bubbly Brazilian spirit.

Don't miss the opportunity to join in the fun; it's by far the best way to experience what it feels like to be part of this vast, vibrant country.

Flashback

Early History

Between 20,000 and 30,000 years ago, waves of nomadic hunter-gatherers crossed over the Bering Strait from Asia—linked by land to North America—in search of food and warmer climes. By 10,000 BC some of them had reached the Amazon basin.

The tribes became widely scattered and never evolved into the remarkable Indian civilizations found in Mexico or the Andes, such as the Maya and Aztec. Instead, they consolidated hunting and fishing with agricultural development, cultivating crops that are still Brazilian staples, like manioc and sweet potato.

As many as 5 million Indians, in hundreds of separate tribes, inhabited the land that is now Brazil. Their culture remained virtually unchanged until the advent of European exploration and colonization at the beginning of the 16th century.

Portuguese Discovery

Even before they discovered it officially in 1500, the Portuguese already owned Brazil in theory. Under the 1494 Treaty of Tordesillas signed with Spain, all territories up to 370 leagues west of the Cape Verde Islands belonged to the Portuguese. This gave them the bulbous, eastern chunk of the South American continent without their even knowing it existed.

Paradoxically, it was Portugal's interests in India that led to the first landing in Brazil. A large fleet under Pedro Alvarez Cabral set sail, with the intention of reaching India via the Cape of Good Hope at the tip of Africa. But in trying to avoid the calm waters of the Gulf of Guinea, it sailed so far west that, on April 22, 1500, the coast of Brazil was sighted. Claimed immediately for the Portuguese crown, it was named Terra de Vera Cruz (Land of the True Cross).

At first, the new possession didn't seem promising enough for permanent settlement. The Indians living there in Stone Age conditions were an unlikely market for rich merchandise, and there was none of the gold and spices that the Portuguese had dreamed of. The only valuable commodity they could find was *pau-brasil*, a wood from which red dye could be extracted, and because of the importance of trade in this substance, the country quickly came to be known in Portugal as Brasil.

The First Colonists

It wasn't until 1533 that the first organized attempt to settle Brazil took place, mainly as a response to the French muscling in on the brazilwood trade. Colonists were sent from Portugal with animals and plants to establish a series of 15 hereditary "captaincies". Many of these withered over the ensuing years, unable to resist attacks by Indians or French pirates. Finally, in 1549, King João III of Portugal decided to centralize authority under a military governor. The first holder of the office, Tomé de Sousa, founded Salvador as the capital of a unified Brazil, a position the city was to hold for the next 214 years.

Colonial Era

After establishing themselves in the new land, the Portuguese soon set about coercing the Indians to work on their sugar plantations. But apart from the fact that they were evidently unable to adapt to plantation life, the Indians had been given partial protection by the Crown as early as 1574, when João III decreed that all Indians be fully in the care of the Jesuits. The plantation owners still needed labour, however, and the result was a rapid increase in the number of African slaves brought into Brazil from the mid-16th century onwards. Initially they worked on the sugar plantations but eventually picked cotton and coffee, panned for gold, and worked as cooks, porters, labourers, artisans and even soldiers. It is fair to say that African slave labour largely built and maintained colonial Brazil.

During the 17th century, Brazil began to expand westwards from the coast. The most daring, and brutal, pioneers were the *bandeirantes* (flag-carriers), who set out from São Paulo on great treks, or *bandeiras*, consisting of anything from 100 to 3,000 settlers and lasting for years at a time. They penetrated to the Uruguayan border and up into the Mato Grosso and Amazon regions, seeking gold and waging bloody war on any Indians they found, even those protected by the Jesuit missions. They had a vital influence on Brazil's future, as they extended the country's boundaries to reach halfway across the interior of South America.

The 18th Century

Europe's sweet tooth had ensured that the sugar trade brought incredible wealth to the northeast. However, a vast deposit of gold was discovered in Minas Gerais in 1693, and in the wake of a dramatic rush to the region, the economic and political centre gravitated southwards. Throughout the century, gold was channelled down to Rio de Janeiro, which consolidated its position as Brazil's premier city by becoming the capital in 1763. From Rio, much of the gold found its way to England in exchange for manufactured goods, and thus Brazil played a significant part in kick-starting the Industrial Revolution.

Vast wealth was being generated in Brazil, but many Brazilians began to feel that it was the Portuguese who unfairly benefited through their control of taxation and the political system. It was time for a change, and revolution was in the air.

Independence

The most celebrated challenge to Portuguese rule came in Ouro Prêto, the town at the heart of the gold mines in Minas Gerais. In 1792, a group of prominent middle-class citizens headed a conspiracy to overthrow colonial rule. They were betrayed, however, and one of them—known as Tiradentes, "the tooth-puller", because of his dentistry skills—was singled out by the authorities for terrible punishment: he was hanged, drawn and quartered in Rio. He quickly became, and remains to this day, Brazil's greatest national hero.

Independence finally came 30 years later. When Napoleon invaded Portugal in 1807, the Portuguese king transferred his entire court of some 15,000 to Brazil under the protection of the British fleet, and the colony found itself in the strange position of being the seat of government for the mother country. As a result, Brazil was transformed from colonial backwater to metropolitan sophisticate. The Portuguese trading monopoly was ended, and the ports opened up to other—mainly British—traders. Although Napoleon was defeated in 1815, João VI had succumbed to Brazil's charms enough to stay on for six more years, at which point he could no longer ignore the demands at home for his return. His son Pedro, ordered by his father to stay on in Rio as vice-regent, sensed that the Brazilian people weren't ready to go back to direct rule from Lisbon after their taste of political maturity, and a year later, on September 7, 1822, he declared Brazil an independent empire, titling himself Emperor Dom Pedro I.

It was a remarkably peaceful revolution. Whereas Spanish America broke up into separate republics through the strain of fighting for independence, Brazil moved into the new era bloodlessly and intact.

The Empire

Pedro I proved a disappointment to his people. After a disastrous war with Argentina, which re- 9

The Amazonian Indians that have survived in the forest still cling to their ancient culture, sleeping in hammocks and hunting with bow and arrow.

sulted in the loss of Brazil's southernmost province of Cisplatina (now Uruguay), he abdicated in favour of his five-year-old son.

Pedro II's reign, lasting almost 50 years, is considered Brazil's golden age. Pedro was democratic and modern-minded, and gave the country a much-needed period of stability, encouraging decent government, modern communications and transport. Unfortunately he did nothing about slavery, which remained legal until 1888, later than any other American country. This issue proved to be his eventual undoing. Maintaining slavery had kept the support of the big land-owners, but they blamed Pedro when the abolitionists finally carried the day, especially for not receiving compensation. Without the backing of the landowners he was unable to control the army, who also had grievances. A military revolt on November 15, 1889 led to the Emperor's abdication and the setting up of a republic.

The Republic

Brazil's first presidents were, in reality, military rulers. Favouring modernity over religion, they disestablished the Catholic Church from the state. Brazil's most important commodity was now coffee, which meant that economic power moved to the coffee region around São Paulo. This brought a huge influx of Europeans into the south, especially Germans and Italians, as well as Japanese immigrants to work on the coffee plantations.

In the 1920s, however, overall economic failure caused considerable unrest in the country. There were further, unsuccessful military coups, but the army finally flexed its muscles to good effect when it refused to accept the outcome of the 1930 election that made the coffee growers' candidate president; the resulting revolution put the opposition candidate, Getúlio Vargas, in power instead.

The Vargas Era

Getúlio Vargas was a nationalist-populist who, like Perón in Argentina, drew support from the working class and labour movements, and focused political resentment on the landowners and their slavish following of European culture. Vargas was to dominate Brazilian political life for the next 20 years.

During World War II, Brazil supported the Allies and was the only South American country to send troops to fight in Europe. However, immediately after the war Vargas was overthrown by the army. He returned to power in the 1950 elections, but following a political corruption scandal in 1954, the military forced him to resign. He committed suicide the same day.

Modern Nation

Vargas's political heir, Juscelino Kubitschek, was instrumental in setting the tone of modern Brazil. He was the driving force behind ambitious development plans such as the construction of highways and hydroelectric plants, though he piled up the national debt by taking on vast foreign loans to pay for them. His greatest memorial is Brasília, inaugurated as the new capital in 1960.

Rampant inflation and political unrest made the re-establishment of military rule inevitable in 1964. But in the wake of nationwide demonstrations demanding elections, a civilian president was once again running the country by 1985.

Almost 90 million Brazilians took part in the 1994 election that put the previous finance minister, Fernando Henrique Cardoso, into the office of president. His plans to link the Brazilian currency to the US dollar and liberalize the economy had been credited with an upturn in Brazil's economic situation. He was re-elected in October 1998 for another four-year term. Democracy, it seems, has taken root again in this "land of the future".

The Southeast

The Southeast is Brazil's economic powerhouse, containing the nation's three largest cities and almost half its population. Made up of four states—Rio de Janeiro, São Paulo, Minas Gerais and Espírito Santo—the region produces vast amounts of minerals, coffee and high-energy excitement. Visit Rio for the world-famous Carnival, São Paulo for its cosmopolitan cuisine, and the town of Ouro Prêto in Minas Gerais for a glimpse of colonial Brazil. The Southeast is probably where you'll first set foot in Brazil—the problem will be tearing yourself away.

RIO DE JANEIRO

City Centre, Zona Sul, Zona Norte, Niterói, Excursions

Visitors to Rio might be forgiven for feeling a touch of jealousy towards the Cariocas, as its inhabitants are known. Clustered round the deep blue waters of Guanabara Bay, with the Sugar Loaf Mountain standing sentinel at the harbour entrance and the famous statue of Christ looming high on the Corcovado peak behind it, their city is simply the most breathtaking in the world. Add to this the superb white beaches fringed with palms, an average temperature that rarely dips below 20°C (68°F), the pervasive atmosphere of Carnival, and the style and sassiness of the people themselves, and you can only agree with your hosts that this is indeed the *Cidade Maravilhosa* —the Marvellous City.

Although São Paulo has now overtaken Rio in terms of wealth and population, and the capital has moved to Brasília, Cariocas know that whatever happens, wherever their city goes today, the rest of the country will follow tomorrow.

City Centre

Getting around Rio is easy. There's an efficient, safe metro system and a network of buses

Rio's favelas are best seen from afar.

with destinations clearly marked on the front and side. Downtown Rio's main artery, Avenida Rio Branco, is a good place to begin exploring.

Praça Floriano

At the southern end of Avenida Rio Branco, this is one of Rio's most impressive squares. On one side, Cinelândia is a lively area of bars, cafés and, as its name suggests, cinemas. The north of the square is dominated by the splendid Teatro Municipal. Opened in 1909, it's a scaled-down version of the Paris Opéra-Garnier. The

---

HARSH REALITY

Perched precariously on Rio's steep hillsides or banished to the outskirts of the vast São Paulo megapolis, *favelas*, or shanty towns, have been a major blot on Brazil's sunny horizon. In Rio alone, more than 2 million people live in their rickety shacks. Strangely enough, they owe their existence to the region's economic success story. Countless thousands fled to the area from poorer parts of the country, such as the barren *sertão* in the northeast interior, seeking work and a share of the Brazilian dream. But the *favelas* are eloquent reminders that they have yet to find either.

---

mosaic-covered Assyrian restaurant downstairs is well worth a visit.

Across Avenida Rio Branco, the two large neoclassical buildings are the Biblioteca Nacional, dating from 1910, and the Museu Nacional de Belas Artes, housing an especially fine collection of Brazilian art. Look out for some striking canvasses by Brazil's first-rate 20th-century artists such as Cândido Portinari's *Café* and Emiliano di Cavalcanti's huge triptych *Navio Negreiro*.

Catedral Metropolitana

Head west along Avenida República do Chile, and the unmistakable Metropolitan Cathedral erupts out of the skyline like a concrete volcano. Also known as the Nova Catedral, the building was completed in 1976. Its cavernous interior is longer than a football pitch and can accommodate 20,000 worshippers. Four gigantic stained-glass windows, one each of green, blue, red and yellow, draw the eye dizzyingly upwards. A plaque at the main entrance commemorates the day Pope John Paul II preached at the cathedral: July 2, 1980.

Largo da Carioca

To the north of the cathedral, on the other side of the cubic Petrobras building (Brazil's national oil company), is the small Largo da Carioca park. Perched on a small hill at the back, the simple, whitewashed Igreja e Convento de Santo Antônio is the oldest, and perhaps the most attractive of Rio's churches. Begun in 1608, it contains fine jacaranda wood-carvings, a sacristry made from Portuguese marble, and *azulejos*, or Portuguese blue tiles, depicting St Anthony's miracles.

For an interesting walk from here, go down Rua da Carioca. At No. 39, Bar Luis, now something of an institution, has been selling beer to thirsty locals since 1887. Originally Bar Adolf, it changed its name during World War II.

Campo de Santana

Heading west through Praça Tiradentes, where the national hero after whom it is named was publicly executed in 1793, you arrive at Campo de Santana, a delightful place to cool off in the shade for a while. It was here that Dom Pedro I proclaimed Brazilian independence. Today, the park supports a substantial population of *agouti*—large, tailless rodents who happily go about their business while ignoring their human neighbours.

Santa Teresa

Close to the Catedral Metropolitana is the *bonde* terminal. The *bonde*, a small, open-sided tram, judders along precipitously over the 18th-century Carioca aqueduct, up narrow cobbled streets and past the old colonial houses of Santa Teresa. There are great views at every turn, but the ride is an experience in itself.

Halfway up the hill, be sure to make the detour to the Museu Chácara do Céu. The museum contains Picasso's *La Danse* and a small collection of modern European masters such as Matisse, Modigliani, Monet and Derain.

Praça XV de Novembro

This was colonial Rio's main square. Its unusual Pyramid Fountain is the work of one of Brazil's leading 18th-century sculptors, Mestre Valentim.

The elegant three-storey colonial building is the Paço Imperial, dating from 1743. Home to the Portuguese viceroys, the palace became the first residence of João VI when he moved his court to Brazil in 1808.

Halfway along Praça XV on the right, the Arco de Teles is an 18th-century arcade leading to narrow, winding streets. Here, you can still savour the atmosphere of old Rio.

Across busy Rua 1° de Março, running north off Praça XV, is a group of baroque churches. On the left, with a tall corner bell-tower, is the church of Nossa Senhora do Carmo da Antiga Sé, the former cathedral, where the

Matchless view from the Sugar Loaf of Rio's bays and beaches.

emperor of Brazil was crowned. The remains of Portuguese explorer Pedro Alvares Cabral are in the crypt. The fine baroque interior is relatively modest compared with the Igreja da Ordem Terceira do Carmo immediately next door. Notice the striking portals, the exuberant decorations on the walls, the rich altar and the marble sculptures, all the work of Mestre Valentim.

Rua 1° de Março ends at Praça Pio X, containing the imposing N.S. da Candelária. Construction of this Italianate domed church took over a hundred years from its foundation in 1775. This was partly because the lavishness of the building nearly broke the bank. The sumptuous interior is decorated with marble of varied colours, and the two huge bronze pulpits are supported by marble angels.

Museo Histórico Nacional

Along the waterfront, the national Historical Museum is housed in the Fortaleza de São Tiago (St James Fortress), one of the few buildings to survive from the 16th century. The museum traces Brazilian history from the arrival of the Europeans. On display are furnishings, thrones and ceremonial trappings from Brazil's colonial and imperial past.

Zona Sul

The area south of the centre has plenty of faded charm and some excellent attractions.

Parque do Flamengo

Before 1960, this lively beach and park area was covered entirely in sea water. In Brazil's biggest landfill programme, some 120 ha (300 acres) were reclaimed from the harbour. Brazil's master landscape architect, Roberto Burle Marx, transformed the new terrain into a precious green belt between the sea and the city, with lots of sporting activities, leisure facilities and places simply to take it easy. The park also contains the Monument to the Unknown Soldier and several museums, including the spectacular Museu de Arte Moderna. The museum has struggled to recover from a fire in 1978 that almost entirely destroyed the original collection, and had already amassed a vast new one of contemporary Brazilian art.

Overlooking the park is the delightful little church of N.S. da Glória do Outeiro, built in the 1720s. The interior walls are decorated with Portuguese *azulejos*.

Museu da República

Continue south along Rua do Catete. Near the Catete metro is one of the best museums in the country, the Museu da República.

Completed in 1866 for a rich coffee baron, the building was used as the Presidential Palace from 1897 until Brasília became the capital in 1960. The façade is suitably impressive, with five great bronze eagles standing on the balustrade over the entrance. The museum concentrates on Brazil's years as a republic. On show are portraits and memorabilia of the nation's presidents, the state rooms where foreign dignitaries and influential Brazilians were entertained, and on the top floor an exhibition devoted to the celebration of modern Brazilian culture. It was in a bedroom in this palace that the charismatic president Getúlio Vargas committed suicide in 1954. The room where where he shot himself has been arranged to look as it did on that day, with the fatal bullet illuminated in its own showcase.

Next door, the Museu Folclorico Edison Carneiro brings together folk art and artefacts such as musical instruments, ceramics, Afro-Brazilian cult pieces and toys from around the country.

Sugar Loaf

Visible from anywhere in Zona Sul, Sugar Loaf is one of the most distinctive mountains in the world. Composed of solid granite, it stands 394 m (1,293 ft) above Guanabara Bay. The Indians called it *pau-nh-acuqua*, meaning "high peak". The sound of the Indian name and the mountain's shape reminded the Portuguese of a *pão de açúcar*, a loaf of refined sugarcane.

Unless you're a dedicated mountaineer, the only way up is by cable car, which makes the journey in two stages. The trip begins at the Estação do Teleférico. At the first station there's a restaurant with live music and samba evenings, shops and a curious little museum of mechanized marionettes. A second car leaves for the summit. The planes taking off at Santos Dumont airport look like models, and Rio is spread out before you like a map. A good time to be here is sunset.

Copacabana

Rio's beaches are justifiably world-renowned. But they aren't only for tourists. You'll find that most of the people who colonize them are Cariocas, for whom they are not so much an escape as a way of life. To get here, you can take any number of Rio's wildly driven local buses.

With a name that launched a thousand nightclubs, Copacabana is the most famous of them all. Its dramatic curve of white sand stretches 4.5 km (almost 3 miles), with Sugar Loaf towering over one end and the Museu e Forte de Copacabana at the other. The beach itself is a forest of goal-posts, volleyball nets and exercise frames, all dedicated to showing off the body beautiful. The wide promenade, paved with an undulating pattern of black and white stones, is crammed with joggers, cyclists, roller-skaters and sightseers. There are plenty of cafés serving up refreshing *chopp* (ice-cold draft beer), or refrigerated coconut milk to be drunk straight from the shell.

Ipanema

On the other side of the southern peninsula lies Ipanema beach. Close to the rocky outcrop is a good surfing area, where huge waves crash in off the Atlantic. Nearby, a hilly municipal park named Praça Garota de Ipanema (Girl From Ipanema Plaza) honours the song, and the girls, responsible for the area's fame. Venture into Ipanema's streets, just back from the beach, to discover Rio's most chic boutiques, as well as many of its best bars and restaurants.

Other beaches

The Cariocas have moved relentlessly on in pursuit of new beaches. The further along the coast you go, the quieter they become. You can reach Pepino and São Conrado by bus. Praia Barra da Tijuca is 12 km (7 1/2 miles) out and very fashionable with Rio's weekenders.

Ipanema love story. "But each day when she walks to the sea, she looks straight ahead, not at he…"

Tijuca National Park

If it's tropical rainforest you want to see, you don't even have to leave Rio. During its early colonial development, the forests that covered the Tijuca mountainsides were felled for lumber and the land used for sugar and coffee plantations. A reforestation programme was undertaken in the middle of the 19th century and a natural wilderness revived at the heart of the city. Today, you can take excellent hikes in the Parque Nacional, where there are waterfalls, caves, and several impressive viewing points. Look out for agoutis, ocelots, monkeys, and exotic birds.

Jardim Botánico

Just south of the national park, towards the coast, lies Rio's Botanical Garden. In 1809 the *Palma Mater*, mother of all the royal palm trees in Brazil, was planted here; the seeds had been taken from Mauritius. Avenues of descendant royal palms still tower over all the other inhabitants of this garden and forest. Among other highlights: six lakes, including a pond in which enormous Victoria lilies float like platters on a tabletop; the orchid nursery; a special hothouse for insectivorous plants; and Mestre Valentim's sculpture *Ninfa do Eco* (Echo Nymph).

19

Corcovado

You will inevitably be drawn to the "Humpbacked Mountain". At more than 715 m (2,326 ft), with its wide-ranging views and statue of Christ the Redeemer with outstretched arms, it has become the symbol of modern Rio. Designed by French sculptor Paul Landowski and made of reinforced concrete, the statue stands 30 m (98 ft) tall. A small chapel is built into the base of the monument, which was completed in 1931. Gaze out from the terrace and the entire city spreads below you— the large heart-shaped lagoon at the back of Copacabana, the huge ship-filled harbour and thrusting Sugar Loaf.

The easiest way to get to Corcovado is by the cog-train that leaves from Rua Cosme Velho to make its vertiginous way up through the jungle. For the best views going up, sit on the right-hand side.

Zona Norte

This is a fairly run-down part of Rio, and apart from visiting its few major sights, tourists generally stay away. But it will give you a good idea of how ordinary Cariocas live.

Quinta da Boa Vista

The largest park in Rio is the primary attraction. It's particularly pleasant on a Sunday when local families gather to enjoy pedal-boating on the lake, the city's zoo (Jardim Zoologico), and the excellent National Museum.

Museo Nacional

Housed in a fine, early 19th-century neoclassical palace, home to the royal family for 81 years, the museum was founded by João VI in 1818 and is one of the oldest scientific institutions in Latin America. It specializes in anthropology and the natural sciences, and has an interesting exhibition of dinosaur skeletons and fossils, Indian ceramics and other aspects of Indian culture. There are also items from all of Brazil's regions, including a display of saddles, boots and weapons from the *gaúchos,* Brazilian cowboys. The star exhibit, however, is just inside the entrance hall—a five-ton lump of meteorite that crashed to earth in the state of Bahia in 1888.

Maracaná

The biggest soccer stadium in the world is just a short distance away. Resembling a Roman colosseum for the 21st century, it was rushed to completion in less than two years for the World Cup Finals in 1950. Big games are usually played on Sundays at 5 p.m., in an atmosphere that rivals Carnival for passion and excitement. It's worth going to a match even if you hate football.

Niterói

Tunnels and a bridge stretching over Guanabara Bay connect Rio with the large city of Niterói. This is the site of Oscar Niemeyer's Museum of Contemporary Art, like a flying saucer come to rest opposite the Sugar Loaf. The out-of-this-world museum houses more than 1,000 paintings by the best-known contemporary Brazilian artists, taken from the collection of economist João Sattamini.

Excursions

Here are three worthwhile trips in Rio de Janeiro State.

Petrópolis

Petrópolis lies about 65 km (40 miles) north of Rio. Pedro II, after whom the town is named, established his summer capital here, among the relatively cool hills of the dramatic Serra dos Orgãos.

Don't miss the Museu Imperial. Inaugurated in 1945, the museum is housed in the neoclassical Summer Palace, built a century earlier. Noteworthy paintings, tapestries and furniture fill the building. The most valuable single exhibit, kept under armed guard, is Pedro II's imperial crown. Other paraphernalia of power include the emperor's throne and sword, as well as the regalia of the Order of the Garter conferred on him by Queen Victoria.

Behind a wrought-iron fence in the Catedral São Pedro de Alcântara are the tombs of Pedro II and the royal family.

Angra dos Reis

Along the Atlantic coast west of Rio de Janeiro, this fishing and shipbuilding port dominates a sweeping bay spattered with islands. Angra dos Reis, meaning "Cove of the Kings", makes a handy base for boat trips to pretty islands such as Ilha Grande. The town was founded at the beginning of the 16th century, and there are several interesting old churches, in particular N.S. do Carmo, dating from the late 16th century. Note also the colonial town hall on Praça Nilo Peçanha, built in the early 17th century.

Parati

Beyond Angra dos Reis, Parati is a charming town in which cars are banned and the 17th-century atmosphere is preserved in old cobbled streets and exquisite churches. The town once had a monopoly on the export of gold and diamonds, but when a road was constructed linking Rio to the gold-mining areas, Parati sank back into obscurity. It made good use of its moment of glory, however, and the handsome colonial buildings are set scenically between the green mountains and delightful harbour.

21

SÃO PAULO
City Sights, Santos, Ilhabela

São Paulo is the largest city south of the equator, and Brazil's economic locomotive. Its soaring skyscrapers go on as far as the eye can see, and its people, known as Paulistanos, are always on the move, wheeling and dealing their way through its crowded streets from morning till night. Forget samba—this city dances to the tune of mobile phones, business talk and money.

Despite its modernity, a frontier spirit lives on. The Paulistanos are proud of their pioneering past, when the courageous, ruthless *bandeirantes* set out from here to conquer Brazil's interior. In the 19th century, huge fortunes were made from coffee, which easily took root in São Paulo's fertile *terra roxa* (red earth).

With waves of immigration from Germany, Italy and Japan at the beginning of the 20th century, the city's economic position only strengthened, developing into an industrial and technological centre after World War II. If they could come back today, the two Jesuit priests who set up a mission station and school here in 1554 would be amazed to see the megapolis of almost 20 million people that it has become.

City Sights
Although its size is daunting, São Paulo comes as a pleasant surprise. Travelling around is easy, thanks largely to the excellent metro system. Parks and museums dot the city, and its cosmopolitan background means there is a plethora of restaurants providing top cuisine from around the world.

Praça da Sé
Fountains, eye-catching sculptures, tall palms and a lively market fill Cathedral Square. The monumental neo-Gothic cathedral, completed in 1969, has a grandiose interior capable of holding 8,000 worshippers.

Capela de Anchieta
The city's founding fathers, José de Anchieta and Manuel de Nobrega, built São Paulo's first church on a site just north of Praça da Sé. This whitewashed chapel in the Pátio do Colégio is a beautiful reconstruction of the 16th-century original. The Museu Padre Anchieta next door has old documents and other relics relating to the first settlement.

São Paulo's streets are constantly thronged with people.

Solar da Marquesa de Santos

As you leave the chapel, the small road to the left brings you to the peach-coloured home of the Marquesa de Santos, one of the few surviving colonial buildings in São Paulo. The Marchioness was Dom Pedro I's mistress, and bore him five children. The house now contains the city museum.

Mercado Municipal

The German-built Municipal Market, Rua da Cantareira 306, was completed in 1933. Inside the main entrance are five splendid stained-glass windows, depicting rural scenes that look distinctly Middle-European.

Praça da República

The square was once home to the great mansions of São Paulo's coffee barons. It now has a market, a tourist information booth, and two important modern buildings. The landmark office-block, Edifício Itália, is a 41-storey corner building with an observation terrace at the top. Nearby is the singular wave-shaped Edifício Copan, a residential building designed by Oscar Niemeyer in 1951.

Teatro Municipal

Rua Barão de Itapetininga, a noisy shopping precinct opposite the square, leads to the remarkable Teatro Municipal. Built at the beginning of the century on the back of the coffee boom, this superb mixture of Art Nouveau and neo-baroque has a sumptuous interior decorated in marble, onyx and bronze, and remains a premier venue for concerts.

Viaduto do Chá

Further along is the Tea Viaduct, crossing the Vale do Anhangabaú where tea was once grown. Today it's an enjoyable pedestrians-only spot, full of buskers and hawkers.

Memorial da America Latina

Outside the Barra Funda metro station, this building is as much a memorial to high-modernist architecture as to the people of Latin America. Designed by Oscar Niemeyer, the complex contains a Latin-American study centre, concert theatre and exhibition hall. A giant concrete hand greets you at the entrance. Great, gleaming white structures, with Niemeyer's hallmark curves, are dotted about the compound. Inside the Salão dos Atos, Cândido Portinari's anguished painting *Tiradentes* is an epic portrait of the nation's hero.

Museu de Arte de São Paulo

The MASP, as it's generally known, on fashionable Avenida Paulista, is without doubt the best museum in the city. In its possession are works by Van Gogh, El Greco, Goya, Picasso, Velasquez and several French Impressionists, as well as exceptional canvasses by Portinari and many others, but they are not necessarily all on display, as the gallery tends to concentrate on temporary exhibitions. Check first before you go in.

Parque do Ibirapuera

Landscaped by Roberto Burle Marx, with buildings designed by Oscar Niemeyer, Ibirapuera is no ordinary park. It boasts a planetarium, sports facilities, a Japanese pavilion and several important museums.

The Museu de Arte Contemporânea has an impressive collection of 20th-century works. The sweeping curves of the nearby Museu de Arte Moderna again betray Niemeyer's distinctive style; the art on display is mainly Brazilian. Just outside the main entrance stands Victor Brecheret's epic sculpture, *Bandeiras*. This monument to the early pioneers captures in stone the sense of their relentless venturing spirit.

Instituto Butanta

Out in the western sector, the institute is home to thousands of snakes, poisonous spiders and edgy-looking scorpions. There's also a museum and research centre, where snakes are milked for their venom to make serum.

Not far from here, you can see an example of a typical pioneer homestead of the 18th century, the Casa do Bandeirante.

SUSHI IN THE TROPICS

In 1908, 830 Japanese immigrants, mainly farmers, arrived at Santos harbour. Escaping terrible crop failures at home, they had come to make their fortunes in the coffee-boom state of São Paulo. By the 1950s, another 250,000 of their compatriots had joined them, and today São Paulo has the largest Japanese community outside Japan.

The centre of Japanese life in São Paulo is the Liberdade district, just south of Praça da Sé. Here, you will find Japanese businesses, hotels and any number of excellent restaurants. Walking around the streets of Liberdade, you'll have to remind yourself constantly that you're not in Tokyo.

Be sure to visit the fine Museu Histórico da Imigração Japonesa, which has informative displays on the history of the Japanese community in Brazil.

Santos

Sprawling along the Atlantic coast, 75 km (46 miles) south of São Paulo, Santos is South America's biggest port. Vast quantities of Brazilian produce fill the voluminous warehouses lining the wharves. Founded in 1535, Santos is one of the oldest settlements in Brazil, although there's not much left of its colonial past. The most interesting building is possibly the railway station, dating from 1867 and looking as though it had been transplanted from a provincial English city. Good restaurants (try the seafood), some fine panoramic views and a change of pace make this a highly enjoyable day trip from São Paulo.

Ilhabela

This large island of 340 sq km (131 sq miles) is the "in place", off the coast between Santos and Rio. At weekends and on holidays, hordes of Paulistanos take the ferry to its glistening shores, filling to the brim the hotels and bars, hiking through the jungle and swimming in pools fed by waterfalls. Ilhabela village at the northeastern end of the island has many fine colonial buildings and a well-restored 17th-century church, Nossa Senhora da Ajuda e Bom Sucesso.

If you want to do something different, rent a horse and buggy and visit the Feiticeira plantation with its underground cells and fortifications. The journey along the coastal road affords superb views. Don't miss the Pedras do Sino, or Bell Rocks, which make a shrill ringing sound when struck with a stone.

The best beaches are on the Atlantic side, many reachable only by boat. Make sure you have plenty of insect repellent.

WHISTLING DIXIE

Of all Brazil's 19th-century immigrants, the most intriguing were perhaps the Confederates from the American South. After their defeat in the American Civil War, many exiled themselves from the new, slave-free America, and settled near São Paulo. As most of them had been plantation cotton-growers in the steamy south, the climate, crops and politics of this part of Brazil—where slavery was legal until 1888—made it very much a home from home. Eventually, most returned to the States, but there are still English-speaking descendants in the area. Two settlements survive just north of São Paulo, at Americana and Santa Bárbara d'Oeste, where there is an informative Museu de Imigração covering this historical curiosity.

ESPÍRITO SANTO
Vitória, Domingos Martins

Espírito Santo once benefited from the overflow of wealth at the Minas Gerais mines. At the end of the 19th century, German and Swiss immigrants settled in the mountains and developed a large farming industry. Today the state derives its income mainly from the export of iron ore, timber and coffee.

Vitória
Founded in 1551, Vitória is located on a small island in a bay where the Great Escarpment meets the sea. The town is filled with shops and boutiques, outdoor cafés and leafy squares.

Palácio de Anchieta
Overlooking the port, the former Jesuit mission is one of the few original colonial buildings left in the city. It's now the state governor's residence and closed to the public, but a side entrance gives access to the tomb of Padre Anchieta, co-founder of São Paulo.

Cathedral
The gleaming neo-Gothic spires of the cathedral, a short stroll to the east, loom over the town. Decorated with ornate *azulejos*, the church also has some fine stained-glass windows.

Vila Velha
An enjoyable ferry ride across the bay takes you to the Old Town. The fortified Convento da Penha is reached by an almost vertical walk, but the superb view of Vitória from the top makes the effort worthwhile. The convent, beautifully restored, was established in 1558. The image of N.S. da Penha (Our Lady of the Rock) in the chapel is a major object of veneration, and at Easter some people struggle all the way up the hill on their knees to worship it.

Beaches
The white-sand beaches at Vila Velha and Praia da Costa are among the most pleasant in the whole country. Further south, Guarapari boasts a unique black beach of monazitic sands, reputed to be therapeutic cures for rheumatism and other complaints.

Domingos Martins
A scenic drive from the coast into the hills takes you to Domingos Martins, 41 km (28 miles) from Vitória. A pleasant, peaceful place, the town's main interest is its German architecture and customs preserved from the time of the first immigrants in the 1840s. A small museum evokes the German exodus.

MINAS GERAIS
Belo Horizonte, Ouro Prêto

Minas Gerais (in English, the banal "General Mines") is a landlocked, mountainous state, whose resilient people once carved the most beautiful cities in Brazil out of its unyielding terrain. It was all due to one thing—gold. When the gold rush began in the 1690s, this was one of the most remote regions in the country. The influx of Paulistanos, Indian and African slaves, and fortune-seekers from the northeast caused the mining camps to explode into boom towns. Luckily, some of the vast wealth was lavished on the towns themselves. Minas Gerais remains a wealthy state, and today has one of the fastest-expanding economies in Brazil. It doesn't live in the past, for all its wealth of history.

Belo Horizonte

Ringed by the mountains of the Serra do Curral, and with a year-round temperate climate, the small village of Curral del Rey was a perfect spot for Brazil's first planned city, inaugurated in 1897 as the new state capital. Phenomenal growth since 1945 has made Belo Horizonte the third-largest city in the country, and the centre of the state's mining, agricultural and manufacturing industries. It is notable for its modern architecture, straight, wide avenues, and a very lively nightlife, with several good bars and restaurants.

Downtown

Praça Sete is the hub of the downtown area, filled with banks and businesses, cafés and cinemas. Southeast along Avenida Afonso Pena, the Parque Municipal is one of the city's few green spots. On the edge of the park stands the Palácio das Artes, with theatre venues, galleries devoted mainly to Brazilian art, and a handicrafts centre. On Sunday mornings, an extensive market, Feira de Arte e Artesano, is set up between Rua da Bahia and Rua dos Guajajaras, selling everything from semi-precious stones and jewellery to T-shirts and alarm clocks.

Museu Histórico Abílio Barreto

This 1883 *fazenda* (plantation house) is just about all that's left of Curral del Rey. The museum displays old photographs of the area, furniture and other odds and ends from the period.

Pampulha

A must for fans of modern architecture, the Pampulha district to the north of the city is another creation of Oscar Niemeyer and Roberto Burle Marx. The church of São Francisco de Assis, begun in 1943, is the product of a remarkable collaboration of Brazil's best 20th-century artists. Niemeyer's design—bunker-like white arcs for the main body of the church and a tall, triangular peg for the bell-tower—is strikingly avant garde. Cândido Portinari's paintings of the 14 Stations of the Cross, João Ceschiatti's bronze font, and Burle Marx's landscaping complete the effect. For years after it was built, the Catholic Church refused to hold services here, finding it too unconventional for their taste, and possibly sacrilegious as well.

Ouro Prêto

A winding road through the mountains leads to this baroque jewel. The first sight is like a mirage, for it seems unimaginable that such a bewitching city of tiled red roofs and magnificent churches could be built in such a remote place. But Ouro Prêto, meaning "black gold", was the epicentre of the 18th-century gold rush. Minas Gerais produced 80 per cent of the world's gold during that period, and Ouro Prêto's population was around twice that of New York. In the 1790s, the town became the focus of a major conspiracy to oust the Portuguese. When one of the plotters, the famous Tiradentes, was executed in Rio, his severed head was displayed in Ouro Prêto's main square, which now bears his name.

Escola de Minas

Built in the 1740s, the Escola de Minas, on the north side of Praça

GENIUS OF THE BAROQUE

The outstanding artist of colonial Brazil was Antônio Francisco Lisboa, known by the nickname Aleijadinho, or "Little Cripple". Born in Ouro Prêto in 1738, the son of a Portuguese settler and a slave, he became a master of rococo wood and stone carving, and his work demonstrates a remarkable artistic power. In early middle-age, he developed a severely crippling illness, possibly leprosy, through which he lost the use of his fingers. Utterly dedicated to his art, he continued sculpting, and for the last 30 years of his life worked with chisel and hammer strapped to his wrists. He died in 1814 and was buried in N.S. da Conceição in Ouro Prêto. His work can be seen in the churches of Minas Gerais's exquisite historic cities: Ouro Prêto, Sabará, Congonhas, São João del Rey and Mariana.

Tiradentes, was once the governor's palace. It is now an important mining school. Inside is a museum with a vast collection of mineral ores, crystals and precious stones.

Museu da Inconfidência

At the opposite end of the square, the handsome former town hall has been resuscitated as the Inconfidência Museum. It has some excellent sculptures by Aleijadinho, as well as other items from the town's heyday. But the main exhibit is the Tiradentes section. On display are his death warrant, a part of the gallows used for his execution, his tomb and those of fellow conspirators, put here in the 1930s under the regime of President Vargas.

Churches

The city's 18th-century churches are famous for their rich baroque interiors and the profusion of work by the sculptor Aleijadinho and his father Manuel Francisco Lisboa.

The delightful church of N.S. de Carmo, the highest in the city, was designed by Manuel Lisboa in 1766 and was also worked on by his son. Be sure to look at the baptismal font, one of his great carvings.

Igreja São Francisco de Assis is one of Brazil's most handsome colonial churches, designed by Aleijadinho and containing an abundant amount of his work. The soapstone exterior, and the wood and soapstone carvings inside, are a towering achievement. The trompe-l'œil ceiling by Manuel da Costa Ataíde took nine years to complete; false columns blur with the real ones leading to a painted blue sky that makes it seem as though the church has an open roof.

Antônio Dias was the first prospector to discover gold in Ouro Prêto, and his wealth paid for the church named after him, N.S. da Conceição de António Dias. Manuel Lisboa designed it in 1727, and Aleijadinho was buried in it nearly 90 years later. The sacristry has a museum dedicated to the sculptor's work.

Constructed by slaves during the 1740s, the church of Santa Efigênia dos Prêtos is located on a hill to the east of the town. The money to build it was provided by the slaves themselves, mostly in the form of fractional amounts of gold they smuggled out of the mines—the women hid it in their hair and washed it out in the font.

Igreja Matriz N.S. do Pilar was built in the 1720s. The church is extravagantly gilded, with painted ceilings, elaborate pulpits and six large chandelier-holders in the shape of birds. The altar was carved by Francisco Xavier de Brito.

The South

Comprising three states, Paraná, Santa Catarina and Rio Grande do Sul, the South is European in outlook and agricultural in character. Boosted by huge waves of German and Italian farmers in the late 19th century, the region became highly developed. This is where the country's cattle is bred, wheat and coffee grown, and wine produced. Modern industrial developments have only compounded the region's economic strength. With natural wonders such as the Iguaçu waterfalls and legendary people like the gauchos, Brazil's cowboys, the South is another world, just waiting to be explored.

PARANÁ

Curitiba, Paranaguá,
Vila Velha State Park, Iguaçu Falls

Curitiba

The capital of Paraná state represents Brazilian town-planning at its best. This is a spacious, modern metropolis with room to move, plenty of greenery and unpolluted air, a large pedestrian zone at its heart and an excellent public transport system. Rio may well be the city of your dreams, but Curitiba is the type of place most people would really want to live in.

Argentina has the lion's share of the famous falls, but Brazil commands the grandest view.

Passeio Público

The beautiful city park, laid out close to the centre of town in 1886, is a popular haunt with Curitibanos. You can go boating on its lake, visit the botanical garden and zoo, admire the jewel-like fish in the aquarium, or simply stroll in the cool shade of its tall trees.

Rua XV de Novembro

The city's principal shopping area, with a lively mix of boutiques and restaurants, is all the more pleasant as the civilized city planners have pedestrianized the entire length.

35

Museu Paranaense

Housed in a former government building dating from 1916, in a distinctive Art Nouveau style with typically elaborate metalwork, the museum displays an assortment of artefacts detailing the history of Paraná State.

Catedral Metropolitana

Said to be modelled on Barcelona's cathedral, Curitiba's neo-Gothic one was begun in 1894. The interior has a finely carved wooden pulpit.

Setor Histórico

A pedestrian tunnel to the left of the cathedral leads to the Largo da Ordem, a superbly restored historic quarter with cobbled streets, trendy cafés and the city's oldest church, the simple Igreja da Ordem Terceira de São Francisco of 1737. It contains a museum of sacred art. In the same district, the reconstructed N.S. do Rosário was originally a slave-built church dating from the 18th century.

Paranaguá

Located on the huge Paraná Bay, Paranaguá lies 100 km (60 miles) east of Curitiba. Near the waterfront, a former Jesuit college completed in 1755 provides the baroque setting for the Museu de Arqueológia e Etnológia. The museum has especially interesting exhibits on Indian culture, and primitive and popular art.

Paranaguá has several attractive old churches: the beautifully

---

CURITIBA TO PARANAGUÁ

Buses to Paranaguá take the old pioneer road, Estrada da Graciosa, finished in 1873, offering excellent views of the Great Escarpment as it drops more than 900 m (3,000 ft) into the coast. But the better way to go is by train. A triumph of engineering, the tracks descend the Serra do Mar through mountains and over deep gorges, twisting and turning past a lovely cascade called Véu de Noiva (Bridal Veil) and through deep-green forests of towering Paraná pine, to offer the most unforgettable train journey in Brazil. For the best views be sure to sit on the left-hand side on the way to Paranaguá.

The trains run daily in January and February, but only at weekends outside these months (although it's worth checking as this is always subject to change). The ordinary train departs at 7.30 a.m. and returns at 4.30 p.m., while a special, air-conditioned tourist train leaves at 9 a.m. and goes back at 3.30 p.m. Journey time is approximately 3½ hours.

restored early 18th-century N.S. do Rosário; São Francisco das Chagras (1741), with noteworthy baroque altars; and São Benedito (1784), originally built for the town's slaves.

Vila Velha State Park

Almost 100 km (60 miles) west of Curitiba, the Parque Estadual de Vila Velha contains a curiosity of nature which more than repays the time it takes to get here. Looming up out of the plateau, like gigantic sculptures, are 23 rock pillars carved out of the red sandstone by millions of years of wind and rain. People have long attempted to find human or animal shapes in them, a game you might like to try as well.

Iguaçu Falls

Situated close to the border with Argentina and Paraguay, the town of Foz do Iguaçu has little of interest, but then it's not what people come for. Reached by the "Cataratas" bus are the famous falls, 20 km (12 miles) to the southeast. Higher than Niagara and wider than Victoria, Iguaçu can justly claim to be the world's most impressive falls. The name comes from a Tupi-Guaraní word meaning "Great Waters". It is here that the Iguaçu River, racing down from the Brazilian highlands, crashes over the edge of the Paraná plateau into a narrow

gorge. In total, 275 cascades, separated by jutting rocks and islands of luxuriant vegetation, plummet down an 80-m (262-ft) precipice that is 3 km (almost 2 miles) wide. The result is spellbinding.

The falls are enhanced even further by the vastness of the surrounding jungle, protected as a national park. This primeval forest is rich in orchids, lianas and tree ferns, multicoloured birds and wild animals.

Brazil lies on one side, Argentina on the other. The Argentinian side is easily reached from Foz via Puerto Iguazú (the Spanish spelling) just over the border. You do not need a visa for the day trip, but you must show your passport.

Brazilian side

The first sight of the falls is incredible. The whole panorama, from the cataract of Santa Maria to the stupendous Garganta del Diablo (Devil's Throat) thunders before you. A two-hour walk along spectacular catwalks takes you dizzyingly close to the tumultuous cascade. The spray sweeps out to soak everything in its path, and the noise of the tumbling water is deafening. Mountains of white froth gush hypnotically in front, swifts dart in and out of the spray, and rainbows hang magically in the air.

37

At this point there's an observation tower, where a lift takes you up to Floriano. From here, a path leads to Porto Canoa where, depending on the state of the river, small boats will take you out above the falls. If the river is not in flood you can even land on a rocky islet for a terrifying look right down into the Devil's Throat, where 14 separate cascades dissolve into a brilliant white mist.

Argentinian side

On the Argentinian side, you can get breathtakingly close to the falls. Two different routes, the Passeios Inferiores and the Passeios Superiores, offer either lower or higher views, and both are excellent. From the lower one you can climb down to the river shore and take a boat the short distance to Isla San Martin. If the river isn't in flood you can even bathe below the Two Sisters cascade. From a platform on top of this large rock, you can almost reach out and touch the dramatic flow.

Itaipú Dam

The joint Brazilian-Paraguayan dam at Itaipú up the Paraná River provides an interesting excursion by bus or by boat. If you go by boat, watch for the marker in the water at the junction of the Iguaçu and Paraná rivers which denotes the meeting point of the three countries, Brazil, Argentina and Paraguay.

At Itaipú, the waters of the Paraná have been diverted through a giant canal on the Brazilian side. The plant is the world's biggest hydroelectric enterprise. With all 20 turbines working, Itaipú has a generating capacity of 12.6 million megawatts—more than the combined capacity of the Aswan dam in Egypt and the Grand Coulee in the US.

Ciudad del Este

For an evening excursion, you can drive from Foz across the "Friendship Bridge" over the Paraná River to the border town of Ciudad del Este in Paraguay, a huge high-pressure duty-free shopping centre with casino.

THE MOST REVERED WATERFALL Of all the cascades created by Brazil's huge rivers, the most spectacular is **Foz do Iguaçu**. For the Tupi-Guaraní, the region's original inhabitants, this was also a place of great spiritual significance. Stand before the wide, awesome curtain of cataracts, and it's easy to understand why.

SANTA CATARINA
Florianópolis, Blumenau, Joinville

Florianópolis
The state capital straddles the mainland and the Ilha de Santa Catarina. Two bridges connect them, the Ponte Hercílio Luz, the longest steel suspension bridge in the country, open to pedestrians and cyclists only, and the 800-m (2,625-ft) Colomo Machado Salles bridge.

Praça XV de Novembro
There are some handsome 19th-century public buildings around the main plaza, where you can cool off beneath an expansive century-old fig tree.

The Catedral Metropolitana, at the top end of the square, dates originally from the 1750s but was remodelled in the 20th century. It houses a life-size Tyrolean wooden sculpture of *The Flight into Egypt*. To the right of the cathedral, as you look down towards the port, stands a pink colonial mansion, the Palácio Cruz e Souza, built around 1780. It now contains the state museum.

Old Port
Around what was once the port—land reclamation has pushed out the seafront—pastel-painted colonial houses with their delicate tracery of white stucco are a reminder of Portugal, as are the lace-makers sitting outside in the sun.

Ilha de Santa Catarina
The main areas of interest are on the island. Blessed with 42 excellent beaches, it has become a favourite holiday resort. Green hills, an exuberance of flowers, and colourful fishing villages add to its allure, and in the centre lies the beautiful Lagoa da Conceição. Beside the calm waters of the lagoon, look out for the baroque church of N.S. da Conceição built in 1730.

On the northern point is the long, friendly Praia dos Ingleses (Englishmen's Beach), separated by a prong of land from the curve of Praia de Canavieras, where boats set off on island tours. On the east coast, Praia do Moçambique has 14 km (almost 9 miles) of unspoilt beach to enjoy, while south of here, Praia da Joaquina is home to the Brazilian surfing championships each January.

Blumenau
The road from Florianópolis to Blumenau follows the picturesque Itajaí River. Approaching Blumenau, you could almost believe you were in the Rhineland. This is the heart of the Ger-

man colony set up in 1850 by Dr Hermann Blumenau. The early settlers must have felt very much at home in this steep valley with its German half-timbered architecture. Blumenau is now a flourishing industrial town, a producer of textiles, fine porcelain and crystal. The homes of Dr Blumenau and Fritz Muller, the naturalist and colleague of Darwin who lived here for 45 years, contain small museums documenting their former owners.

Museu Histórico da Família Colonial

Near Praça Hercílio Luz, this museum takes up two of the oldest surviving settler houses, dating from around the 1850s. Early photographs, furniture, and relics of the indigenous Indians who were driven out by the settlers, tell the story of what happened when the first German immigrants established the colony.

Oktoberfest

Distinctly un-Brazilian, the popular two-week Oktoberfest takes over the town. It's a lively occasion where you can consume German food and beer to your heart's content.

Joinville

Despite its name, Joinville is as Germanic as the rest of the area. Its original site comprised the immense domain given by Dom Pedro II as dowry to his sister when she married the Prince de Joinville, son of the French king Louis-Philippe. He allowed Hamburg lumber merchants to exploit the forests, and the first German settlers arrived in 1851.

Museums

Housed in the Prince de Joinville's elegant palace, dating from 1870, the Museo Nacional da Imigração e Colonização is a useful introduction to the history of the German colony, with many photos and artefacts from the time. In front of the museum, you can't miss the Alameda das Palmeiras, an avenue of towering Imperial palms more than a century old.

The Museu Arqueológico do Sambaqui, a treasure-trove of archaeological discoveries, looks at the lives of the Sambaqui Indians, who once inhabited this area.

São Francisco do Sul

The port which serves Joinville, and was the point of entry for its 19th-century immigrants, is one of the oldest communities in the state. It's an attractive spot, on a small island and with a pleasant old town. The beaches nearby are excellent. Praia Paulos and Praia Ingleses, just a short distance to the east of São Francisco, are especially pleasant.

RIO GRANDE DO SUL

Porto Alegre, Aparados da Serra, Pelotas, Rio Grande

This is gaucho land, where the vast, flat pampas is grazed by cattle herded by cowboys on horseback. The Wild West lives on in Brazil's southernmost state, where men are men and the beef is always barbecued. While you are here, be sure to attend a traditional gaucho show, where through music and dance you will find the cultural heart of these fiercely independent people.

Porto Alegre, the state capital, is situated at the junction of five rivers at the northern point of the gigantic Lagoa dos Patos, a freshwater lagoon hundreds of kilometres in length. Founded by immigrants from the Azores in 1742, the settlement has expanded to become Brazil's sixth-largest city. Nearby Pelotas, the state's second-largest town, is a quiet river port which came into being when air-dried beef industries were developed here in the early 19th century. The town is peppered with neoclassical colonial mansions from those prosperous days. At the mouth of the lagoon to the south, on the Atlantic, lies the town of Rio Grande. In the second half of the 19th century it was an important cattle centre; today it is poor and significantly diminished.

Porto Alegre

The "happy harbour" of the name is a bustling port, one of the most up-to-date in Brazil, handling huge ocean-going ships. It is a modern, industrial city, but with its fair share of interesting museums, parks and squares—not to mention the *churrascarias*.

Mercado Público

Built in 1869 close to the banks of the River Guaíba, the market is a good place to buy gaucho souvenirs such as the paraphernalia of *mate*, the gaucho tea that tastes a bit like hedge-clippings. This is the only Brazilian area where tea is popular. They drink it very strong and from a special gourd through a silver straw.

Museums

West of the market, the Museu de Arte do Rio Grande do Sul specializes in gaucho art.

South from here, next to the modern Italianate cathedral, the Museu Júlio de Castilhos has some unusual exhibits, such as moustache cups that belonged to the one-time state governor.

The Museu da Força Expedicionária Brasileira deals with the little-known role of Brazilian troops in World War II, many of whom came from this region.

Public Buildings

Near the cathedral, note the Palácio Piratini, the state governor's palace dating from 1909, and the baroque-style Teatro São Pedro, built in 1858.

Aparados da Serra

To the north of the state capital, the mountain resorts of Gramado and Canela are havens of fresh air, beautifully scenic trails, comfortable Alpine-style hotels and delicious food. Further north again, the Parque Nacional de Aparados da Serra is one of Brazil's great marvels of nature. The park has a lush araucária pine forest, but the real prize is the awe-inspiring Canyon do Itaimbézinho, where the mountain has been ripped apart to form two sheer walls 700 m (2,300 ft) high.

Pelotas

The pedestrians-only streets of the town centre make for pleasant shopping (the town specializes in cakes and preserved fruits). Have a peek into the Catedral São Francisco, built in 1832. The Museu de Arte Leopoldo Gotuzzo (Rua Marechal Deodoro) displays sculpture and paintings of the local artist as well as European artworks. Outside the centre, surrounded by large gardens, the Museu da Baronesa contains furniture, porcelain and paintings from collections of sundry nobles.

Rio Grande

Here the lagoon is so shallow that at low tide you can walk out as far as a kilometre from the shoreline. When the lagoon swells during the rains, the salty waters bring a plethora of crabs, a great delicacy for the table.

City Centre

Have a look around town at the charming old buildings from more prosperous times. The baroque Catedral de São Pedro (1755–75), however, dates from a full century earlier and is the oldest church in the state.

Museums

The Museu Oceanográfico has a wide range of seashells, whale and dolphin skeletons, and other interesting odd flotsam and jetsam retrieved from the sea.

The old customs house on Rua Richuelo, built by Dom Pedro II, now houses the City Museum. Opposite, the Museu do Departamento Estadual de Portos, Rios e Canais displays the machinery used to build the Barra, the large breakwater south of Rio Grande.

São José do Norte

A pleasant way to while away the time is to take a boat from the waterfront and cross the mouth of the lagoon to this typical fishing village—especially photogenic at sunset.

The Midwest

Until Brasília was built in the 1950s, the region was largely desolate. With a fifth of the country's territory and only a fraction of its population, it still looks pretty empty. Made up of the states of Mato Grosso, Mato Grosso do Sul and Goiás, and the autonomous Distrito Federal (Federal District of Brasília), it is a land of savannah, red earth and scrub known as cerrado. On the western border with Bolivia, the unique Pantanal swampland is one of South America's great wildlife showcases.

BRASÍLIA
Eixo Monumental, Palácio da Alvorada

Brasília is like no other capital, a space-age city built from scratch in 1956. Everything about it is improbable, as if a city had been discovered on the moon. A deserted, red-dust plateau suddenly gives way to a futuristic metropolis designed in the shape of the wings and fuselage of an aeroplane. Buildings with huge spikes on top or great inverted domes confront the eye. The site is so remote that materials and workers for the new capital had to be dropped in by helicopter. Four years later, in 1960, it was ready.

You might well muse on why it ever happened. But for more than two centuries, Brazilian philosophers had been advocating a move inland as the only way to develop the whole country, and the idea was even written into the 1889 constitution. It was not until 1956 that the concept got off the ground, when President Juscelino Kubitschek won unanimous parliamentary approval for his bill that set in place a commission which would plan and build the new city.

The layout was the audacious enterprise of urbanist Lúcio Costa and architect Oscar Niemeyer. Roberto Burle Marx landscaped the spaces between the monuments. By using Brazilian architects to design the capital, Kubitschek wanted to signal that his country had arrived on the world stage.

43

Brasília's Catedral Metropolitana.
Architect Oscar Niemeyer
attempted to reproduce
the sensual curves of nature
in his designs.

At first the city was hailed as a real-life utopia, but mass migration exceeded all imagined targets. Large satellite shanty towns and proliferating traffic have brought the planners' dreams down to earth with a bang. But it's still difficult not to marvel at the inspired ingenuity of the original designs. In the purple sunset, made all the more panoramic by the altitude at 1,150 m (3,700 ft), it can look strangely ethereal.

Eixo Monumental

The straight line running past the Television Tower to Lake Paranoá is the Monumental Axis, set aside for government and culture. The intersecting arc, called the Eixo Rodoviária (Highway Axis), slices through the housing districts, divided into "superblocks", which are self-sufficient neighbourhoods. The "wings" and "body" intersect, on separate levels, at the Bus Terminal (Estação Rodoviária) around which are situated business, hotel and entertainment facilities. If you stray outside the centre, you'll have to fathom with abbreviations and acronyms: SHIN, for example, means North Individual Housing Sector and SQS means Superquadra Sul, or South Superblock.

Catedral Metropolitana

One of Niemeyer's greatest works, the cathedral is far bigger than it looks, for while the curved struts of the dome rise up like a gigantic crown of thorns, the body of the church is underground. Alfredo Ceschiatti's fine sculptures of the *Four Disciples* stand outside the entrance, and he also crafted the three aluminium angels that float over the congregation inside.

Esplanada dos Ministérios

Just down from the cathedral, the massive green slabs of the min-

---

CULT FIGURE

Dom Bosco was an Italian priest who in 1883 prophesied that a great new civilization would arise in exactly the spot where Brasília was later built. Many consider the city to be the fulfilment of that vision. As a result, more than 400 different cults have sprung up in and around Brasília, which is seen as the "Capital of the Third Millennium". One worth visiting is the Templo da Boa Vontade (Temple of Goodwill). Cult members worship at a large seven-sided pyramid, supporting at its pinnacle what they claim is the world's largest crystal.

Os Candangos, rendering homage to the men who built the capital.

The big white bowl and twin towers of the National Congress.

istry buildings line either side of the road. Each ministry has its own identical glass box, in which Brazil's civil servants swelter for their country.

Palácio dos Arcos

The Palace of the Arches is a pleasing mixture of modern design and classical elegance, surrounded by a lotus pool, in which sits Bruno Giorgi's powerful sculpture *The Meteorite*. Also known as the Palácio do Itamaraty, the building is owned by the Foreign Office and used mainly for diplomatic functions. To visit, you will have to apply 24 hours in advance.

Congresso Nacional

The far end of the Monumental Axis sees the convergence of the executive, legislative and judicial branches of the federal government. Dominating the entire ensemble, the National Congress is noted for the counterpoint of its dome and inverted dome—the only visible parts of the subterranean chambers of the House of Representatives and the Federal Senate. Between them rise twin 28-storey administrative towers.

Praça dos Três Poderes

There is an impressive group of sculptures in the plaza outside the Palace of Justice. Seated immediately in front is a serene modern version of *Justice blindfolded*, sculpted by Ceschiatti. The best-known statue is Bruno Giorgi's *Os Candangos* (The Pioneers), dedicated to the workers who came here to build the new capital. At the back of the plaza, the Pantheon Tancredo Neves contains João Camara's extraordinarily stark mural in black and white on the life of Tiradentes.

Juscelino Kubitschek Memorial
The memorial to the founder of Brasília takes the form of a huge question-mark with a statue of the president inside. Beneath the memorial is a museum dedicated to Kubitschek and his city.

Sanctuário Dom Bosco
Located in Quadra 702 Sul, this remarkable neo-Gothic church has tall pointed-arch windows entirely composed of blue and violet stained glass. The effect, an interior filled with piercing blue light, is mesmerizing.

Television Tower
To put the whole incredible project into perspective, take the lift to the observation level of the 218-m (715-ft) tower and see how Brasília fits into the all-encircling plain. Here and there you'll see an excavation site with the red earth visible like a wound in the tidy green parkland.

Palácio da Alvorada
Acclaimed by many as Niemeyer's masterpiece, the Palace of the Dawn is the official residence of the Brazilian president. The architect is said to have designed its upside-down arches in a single night; President Kubitschek hailed its "lightness, grandeur, lyricism and majesty". It lies on the shore of Lago Paranoá, a man-made lake with a perimeter of 80 km (50 miles) that gives the landlocked citizens a welcome chance to do some boating and fishing.

MASTER BUILDER
Brazil has a taste for daring modern architecture. The architect who set the pace is Oscar Niemeyer. Born in Rio de Janeiro in 1907, he became a Communist and follower of Le Corbusier's brand of rigorous modernism. Niemeyer's buildings express his desire to unite functionalism with aesthetics. Thus his spectacular free-flowing forms grace buildings that might otherwise be rather dull: the Ministry of Education and Health in Rio, and the Ministry of External Relations in Brasília. He will always be known for the daring new capital city he gave Brazil, which he wanted to be "the act of affirmation of an entire people".

49

MATO GROSSO AND MATO GROSSO DO SUL

Cuiabá, The Pantanal, Campo Grande

Mato Grosso and Mato Grosso do Sul were one vast state until 1977 when the government split it neatly in two. Mato Grosso means "thick scrubland". Many of Brazil's remaining Indians live in the region, but it is also another of Brazil's great cattle-rearing areas, with ranches so big the farmers have to get around by plane. Recent development has improved road communications, making settlers desperate to grab land. Unlikely as it may seem, Cuiabá has the fastest growth-rate of any Brazilian city. The region is the gateway to one of the world's most unusual geographical phenomena—the Pantanal.

Cuiabá

With the Amazon to the north and the Pantanal to the south, Cuiabá has been on the edge of civilization since it was founded as a gold-mining town by the *bandeirantes* in 1719. Today it is the capital of Mato Grosso.

The centre of all the action is Praça da República, where you'll find the cathedral, the post office and the Fundação Cultural de Mato Grosso, with three separate exhibitions looking at the region's history, wildlife and people.

West of here, on Praça Moreira Cabral, look out for the rock that indicates you are standing at the exact centre of the South American continent.

The Museo do Indio, or Rondon Museum, documents the Indian tribes of the Mato Grosso, among them the Bororos, Karajas and Xavantes, with fascinating displays of weapons, tools, cooking implements, terracotta dolls and sumptuous feather-bedecked costumes. It is located at the university, on Avenida Correia da Costa.

Chapada dos Guimarães

Tours are organized in Cuiabá to visit this mountain chain 75 km (46 miles) to the northeast. The national park of 33,000 ha (127 sq miles) is riddled with gorges and has stunning rock formations, 200 waterfalls and fabulous views. At Alta Mira, on the rim of a canyon, a sign points out the "Geodesic Centre" of South America, competing with the one in Cuiabá.

The Pantanal

This vast alluvial plain floods as regularly as clockwork (*pantano* means "swamp" in Portuguese). It was once part of an inland sea, and is as flat as a sea-bed. Each year from October to March, the Paraguai River and its tributaries inundate the land, covering it with up to 3 m (10 ft) of water. The best time to go is in the dry season, from April to September.

The Pantanal is a place that demands some knowledge on the part of its visitors and a great deal of respect. Its fragile ecosystem is greatly threatened by overfishing, poaching of birds, and the expansion of tourism. At 230,000 sq km (88,803 sq miles), spilling over into Bolivia and Paraguay, it's almost half the size of France!

All Creatures Great and Small

The main attraction is the unparalleled chance to observe wildlife in its natural habitat. More than 600 species of bird, 300 types of fish and a variety of land animals live here. Look out for the red-throated jabiru storks, toucans, pink roseate spoonbills, and the noisy parakeets. The water contains such cosy creatures as the alligator, or cayman, and piranha fish. On land, there are capybaras, the world's biggest rodents weighing in at 50 kg (110 lb), howler monkeys, armadillos, tapirs and, less easy to find, jaguars and anteaters. The best place to observe the wildlife is along the Transpantaneira, a dirt road linking Poconé and Porto Jofre.

Campo Grande

The capital of Mato Grosso do Sul, Campo Grande is known for its distinctive dark-red earth and its quantity of cowboy shops. The feel of the American Midwest is enhanced by the grid layout of the streets and the cowboys who flood the town at the weekend.

Dom Bosco Museum

This excellent museum on Rua Barão do Rio Branco is packed with stuffed birds and animals from the Pantanal, insects and butterflies, shells, and exhibits about the local Indians such as the Bororos and Xavantes.

THE TWO BEST TRAIN RIDES The **Curitiba to Paranaguá** Railway takes three hours to descend the 914 m of the Serra do Mar plateau, offering breathtaking views of mountains, gorges and Paraná Bay. For the more adventurous, the **Campo Grande to Corumbá** train skirts the fascinating Pantanal swamp, rubs shoulders with parrots and alligators, and ends up on the Bolivian border.

The Northeast

Composed of nine different states—Maranhão, Piauí, Ceará, Rio Grande do Norte, Paraíba, Pernambuco, Bahia, Alagoas and Sergipe—the Northeast has a variety of splendours on offer. Bahia and Pernambuco were the first major settlements of colonial Brazil. Great sugar plantations were based in the region, and from the 16th century onwards they received vast numbers of African slaves. The forced mixing of cultures has created the Northeast's distinctive flavour, and it still exerts a considerable influence on Brazilian culture. Remote, romantic beaches, the bleakness of the sertão (dry backlands), colonial cities, carnivals and distinctive local delicacies will convince you that this region is indeed the soul of Brazil.

BAHIA
Salvador, Ilhéus, Porto Seguro

Salvador

The city sits on a bluff overlooking the sheltered bay of Todos os Santos, discovered by Amerigo Vespucci on All Saints' Day, November 1, 1501. The wealth that built the city's impressive colonial mansions and baroque churches laden with ornate gold leaf came from the Portuguese sugar plantations of the Recôncavo, the 150 km (90 miles) of

tropical coastline surrounding the bay. Salvador was founded as capital of Brazil in 1549, and remained the centre of political life for more than two centuries.

It lies at the heart of Afro-Brazilian culture. Roman Catholic masses are said alongside African candomblé rituals, Salvador's Carnival competes with Rio's for excitement, and its spicy cuisine is celebrated throughout Brazil.

Praça Municipal

Palácio do Rio Branco, the old governor's palace, now houses the city tourist office. On the bay

Refreshments at the ready outside Nossa Senhora do Bonfim.

side of the square, the Art Deco monument is in fact an elevator. Constructed in 1928, the Lacerda Elevator whizzes you from the upper city (Cidade Alta) to the lower (Cidade Baixa) in seconds. Across Rua da Chile, the arcaded Paço Municipal, the city hall, dates from 1660.

Terriero de Jesus

North of Praça Municipal, the spacious Praça da Sé gives onto another beautiful square still known as Terriero de Jesus, its old name. This square and its environs contain some of Salvador's most delightful buildings such as the cathedral, the 17th-century Dominican church São Domingos, and the 18th-century São Pedro dos Clérigos.

Catedral Basilica

On the west side of the square, the cathedral was completed in 1672 as part of a large Jesuit seminary. The rather austere Portuguese marble exterior gives little hint of what's inside, a breathtaking outburst of rococo and baroque for the altar and 12 side chapels, beneath a splendid carved and gilded wood-panelled ceiling. The walls and ceiling of the sacristy are lined with paintings of Jesuit dignitaries, while the cathedral museum displays a collection of holy images and liturgical objects.

Museu Afro-Brasileiro

Next to the cathedral, what was originally the university's Faculty of Medicine has been restored to house an excellent museum devoted to Bahia's special connection with Africa. Exhibits highlight the various aspects of Afro-Brazilian culture: ceremonial items to do with candomblé, the Bahian religion combining African cults with traits of Catholicism and Brazilian Indian beliefs; Carnival; weaving; African art; music and capoeira, the balletic martial art developed by the slaves.

Igreja São Francisco

On the south side of Praça Anchieta, a continuation of Terreiro de Jesus, stands the 18th-century Church of St Francis, whose opulence would make the eponymous saint blush. The interior is filled with intricate carvings and black-haired cherubs, and covered wall-to-wall in thick gold leaf. In a side altar, Manoel Inácio da Costa's strikingly gaunt São Pedro da Alcântara was carved from a single tree trunk.

Lining one side of the cloister, a wall tiled in Portuguese azulejos relates the marriage of the king of Portugal's son to an Austrian princess, providing an everlasting record of old Lisbon before it was destroyed by earthquake in 1755.

Igreja da Ordem Terceira de São Francisco

Immediately next door, this smaller church is equally impressive. Its riotous Spanish baroque façade encrusted with angels, saints and virgins lay concealed behind a layer of plaster for 150 years, until a painter chipped off a piece by mistake in 1936. The reliquary was redecorated in Art Deco style.

Largo do Pelourinho

Head back to the Museu Afro-Brasileiro and follow the colourful Rua Alfredo de Brito down to Pelourinho, a cobbled square surrounded by colonial mansions, once the site of the pillory where slaves were publicly whipped. What is now the Fundação Casa de Jorge Amado, honouring Brazil's most famous novelist, was once the slave auction house. Down the hill on the right, the eye-catching-blue 18th-century church of N.S. do Rosário dos Prêtos was built by and for slaves, and was originally just outside the city wall.

Today the Pelourinho area bustles with shops, galleries, restaurants and hotels. One of the nicest ways to end the day is with a cold drink on the terrace of the Hotel Pelourinho overlooking the bay.

Igreja do Carmo

The steep incline of Rua Luiz Vianna Filho leads to this baroque church founded in 1636. The church museum contains an odd assortment of objects, but tucked away among the coins, furniture, and other bric-a-brac is a superb statue of *Christ at the Pillar* by Francisco Xavier Chagas, a half-Indian slave with no formal training. Looking closely, you can see that the drops of blood are represented by inlaid rubies.

BALLETIC BATTLE

Originating as an Angolan martial art, *capoeira* has evolved into a stylized, dance-like kung-fu routine between two performers, carried out to the accompaniment of the rhythmic percussion of the *berimbau*. With lots of leaping, swirling and kicking (but not punching—use of hands is not permitted), contestants try to land blows to the beat of the music. In the past, it was a disguised way of settling disputes among slaves as well as training for fighting, presented as a dance so as not to incur the wrath of the slave-owners. You can usually see *capoeira* displays outside Salvador's Mercado Modelo, or else find out about the performances put on at the *capoeira* schools from the Salvador Tourist Office.

Convento de N.S. do Carmo

Next to the Igreja do Carmo, the convent dates from the late 16th century. During the wars against the Dutch in 1624, this was the headquarters of the colonists, and the Dutch surrender was signed here on April 30, 1625. The museum in the sacristy displays an eclectic collection of keys, dinner plates, semi-precious stones and a pillory, and like its neighbour has a Chagas sculpture of Christ.

Cidade Baixa

Very definitely the poor relation, the lower town sprawls out along the waterfront at the bottom of the Cidade Alta's 70-m (200-ft) cliff. Offshore, the sturdy Forte de São Marcelo was built in 1623 to protect the port, and just in time—the following year Salvador was attacked by the Dutch.

Mercado Modelo

Take a look at the covered market at the foot of the Lacerda Elevator. In the noisy, effervescent atmosphere of this huge 19th-century hall, hammocks, jewellery, Bahia dolls, herbs, spices and magic potions are all on sale. In front of the main entrance on the harbour side, there's often a display of *capoeira* taking place.

Igreja NS do Bonfim

In the western suburbs, this is by far the most fascinating of Salvador's 34 colonial churches, with strong links to the candomblé religion. Every day, pilgrims come here in their hundreds to worship the image of Christ (identified with candomblé's most important spirit, Oxala). Every inch of the little museum to the right of the nave is crammed with ribbons, photographs, paintings, messages, football shirts… and even body parts encased in wood, plastic or silver, entreaties for protection during an operation. Every January it is home to the fascinating Lavagem do Bonfim festival, where candomblé and Catholicism take equal part.

Barra

To the south, Barra is an area with beaches, a huge shopping centre, and Bahia's oldest fort, Santo Antônio da Barra, dating from the 1590s. All along this coast to Ilhéus, there are intriguing old colonial settlements and good beaches, such as the renowned sands of Morro de São Paulo on the tiny Ilha de Tinharé.

Ilhéus

Ilhéus nestles at the centre of the cocoa-growing region, and was made famous by Jorge Amado's novel *Gabriela, Clove and Cin-*

Salvador has plenty of good beaches within easy reach.

namon. Amado was born here in 1912, and for those readers hooked by his novels, the family home where it all began is at Rua Jorge Amado 21. Carry on towards the seafront and you'll arrive at the neo-Gothic cathedral, dating from the 1930s. A short walk north of here, the church of São Jorge on Praça Rui Barbosa, is the city's oldest, completed in 1556. Ilhéus is known for its lively festivals, in particular that of St Sebastian in January and the cocoa festival taking up all of October.

Porto Seguro

Monte Pascoal, a mountain to the south of Porto Seguro, was the first part of the country ever to be seen by a European, when Pedro Cabral's fleet arrived off the coast on April 22, 1500. After being entertained by friendly Indians, celebrating mass and claiming the land for Portugal, they departed. Three years later the Portuguese returned, and the column they put in the ground to establish their sovereignty is still there. Look out for the arms of the Portuguese Crown on one side, and Christ's face on the other.

The colonial town overlooks the sea from a high bluff. Cidade Alta has some of Brazil's oldest buildings, including the Misericórdia church, begun in 1526. The nearby Igreja N.S. da Pena dates originally from 1535 and contains an icon of St Francis.

SLAVE NATION

The African slaves in Brazil were rarely resigned to their fate. There were many bloody slave revolts throughout the country, and despite the dreadful punishment meted out to runaways, thousands fled the plantations. These formed into *quilombos*, or slave communities. The largest was the 17th-century Palmares, on the border of present-day Alagoas and Pernambuco. With a population reaching almost 30,000, including Indians and *mestizos* as well as Africans, Palmares was virtually an independent state within Brazil. Its agriculture was more productive than the plantations, and the community was organized like an African kingdom, with a ruler, royal council, army and priest class. The Portuguese sent several armies to destroy this enormous embarrassment to the colonial government. But Palmares survived for 67 years and defeated the Portuguese on numerous occasions, before finally being crushed by a *bandeirantes*-led militia in 1694. Many other *quilombos* followed, but none was as successful as the remarkable Palmares.

PERNAMBUCO

Recife, Olinda, Pernambuco Coast, Maceio

Recife

Built on the islands and peninsulas of two river deltas, and sheltered behind the wall of reefs that gives it its name, Recife likes to flatter itself as the "Venice of Brazil". But the resemblance ends with the bridges, waterways and baroque churches. This is a busy harbour city of over a million people, and the downtown is crowded with modern tower blocks.

Recife has a turbulent past. The Dutch controlled the city in the 17th century, and there have been rebellions against every form of central government since —colonial, imperial and republican. Things are calmer now, though never dull. The city has good museums, a famously raucous Carnival, and, thanks to the huge wealth of its 16th- and 17th-century sugar plantations, no less than 62 historic churches.

Teatro Santa Isabel

At the northern end of Santo Antônio island, Praça da República is the palm-shaded setting for the imposing Teatro Santa Isabel, inaugurated in 1850. A plaque in the main corridor reads: "Here we won the cause for the abolition of slavery." The signatory, Joaquim Nabuco, was a writer and diplomat, and a major force in the abolition movement.

Capela Dourada

Just south of the square, on Rua do Imperador, is the Museu Franciscano de Arte Sacra. You have to walk through the museum to reach the Golden Chapel, the city's most striking sight. The baroque vision in gold was built at the end of the 17th century to show the world that this colonial outpost could rival the architectural splendours of Europe.

Next door, the Franciscan church of Santo Antônio dates from 1606 and is the oldest in Recife. The 18th-century *azulejos* in the church and cloister are especially ravishing.

São Pedro dos Clérigos

Take Avenida Dantas Barreto and head south to this 18th-century church behind whose skilfully sculpted façade lie an indulgence of woodcarvings and an unusual trompe-l'œil ceiling.

Surrounded by boutiques and galleries, Pátio de São Pedro in front of the church forms the heart of Recife's artists' quarter. On Friday and Saturday evenings you can watch impromptu street performances from one of the friendly little outdoor cafés.

Forte das Cinco Pontas

Overlooking the bay at the southern end of the old town, the "five-point fort" was built by the Dutch in 1630. It now houses the Museu da Cidade, displaying maps and old photos of the city and some relics discovered in the fort.

Casa da Cultura de Recife

Opposite the metro station, this is a shopping mall with a difference, very visibly converted from a former prison, with a central atrium and radiating wings. Arts and crafts shops are located in the cells. Music and dance are sometimes performed outside.

Museu do Trem

Next to the station is a good train museum, which reveals the important role the British played during the 19th century in building up Brazil's railways.

Galeria de Arte Metropolitana

Across the Avenida Guararapes bridge on Rua da Aurora 265, the gallery has a startlingly bold collection of paintings by Pernambuco artists, including João Camara Filho's ten brutally satirical canvasses on Brazilian life, *Cenas da Vida Brasileira 1932*.

Museu do Homem do Nordeste

Outside the city centre, at Avenida 17 de Agosto, this is one of the country's best museums, and an excellent introduction to the Northeast. Separate galleries are devoted to the key topics of the region: fishing, religion, indigenous medicine, festivals, ceramics and an unusual section on popular culture that gives serious attention to items such as rum bottles and cigarette packets. As one might expect, given Recife's history, the exhibits on sugar are fascinating and informative.

Boa Viagem

One of Recife's top attractions is its dazzling 10-km (6-mile) beach to the south of the city. Fringed by coconut palms, it's the weekend parade ground of the Recifenses. From the fine promenade restaurants you can watch the fishermen haul their curious log rafts up on the beach after a day at sea.

Olinda

"O linda!" (Oh beautiful!), Duarte Coelho Pereira, the first governor from Portugal, is said to have exclaimed when he arrived at the site of the future settlement of Olinda, on a steep hillside 6 km (4 miles) from Recife. It would be hard to disagree. Founded in 1537, Olinda is a remarkably well-preserved colonial town, with shaded cobbled streets, quiet squares, elegant, pastel-coloured houses and baroque churches.

Olinda's colonial charm has been carefully preserved.

The views across red-tiled roof-tops and tall palm trees to the ocean are breathtaking.

Olinda is where Pernambuco's colonial elite lived, and its fine buildings were paid for by the profits from sugar. A large artistic and literary colony has taken refuge in its old colonial streets.

Around the Cathedral

Alto da Sé (Cathedral Heights) is a good place to get an initial overview of Olinda. The impos-ing cathedral, Igreja da Sé, dating originally from Olinda's founda-tion year of 1537, hides a plain interior. The square has a terrace with cafés, and stalls selling local crafts such as woodcarvings and jewellery. Nearby, the Museu de Arte Sacra is housed in the for-mer Bishop's Palace.

Continue westwards along Rua Bispo Coutinho to reach the attractive Igreja da Misericórdia, founded in 1540. It's the oldest Carmelite church in Brazil, with fine woodcarvings and *azulejos*.

Mercado da Ribeira

The 18th-century slave market, south of Igreja da Misericórdia on Rua Bernado Veira de Melo, now contains painters' studios and art galleries, woodcarving and an-tique shops, and the tourist infor-mation office.

61

Mosteiro de São Bento

At the bottom of Rua São Bento, this monastery was built in 1582 but destroyed by the Dutch 50 years later. It was rebuilt at the end of the 17th century and served for a time as Brazil's first law school. The chapel interior is ornately carved and gilded.

Convento São Francisco

Below the Alto da Sé, to the east, the large complex, founded in 1585, comprises the chapel of São Roque, the church of N.S. das Neves, decorated with wood-carvings in rococo style, and the convent itself.

Pernambuco Coast

The beaches south of Recife are glorious. One of the best is Porto de Galinhas, whose warm waters are sheltered by reefs and fringed with mangroves and palms.

Itamarcá

This lovely island 46 km (29 miles) north of Recife is linked by bridge to the mainland. It is best known for its palm-fringed beaches, Brazil's first sugar mills, the ruins of old naval buildings, and the star-shaped Fort Orange, built by the Dutch in 1631. Rusted cannon still keep watch over the deserted beaches.

Igaraçu

Founded in 1535, Igaraçu was the first European settlement in Pernambuco. Duarte Coelho Pereira built the Igreja dos Santos Cosme e Damião on the site where he defeated the local Potigar Indians, before going on to found Olinda.

Maceio

The capital of Alagoas state lies almost 300 km (186 m) south of Recife. It has several interesting museums: Museo do Folclore Theo Brandão on Praça Sinimbu; Instituto Histórico e Geográfico on Rua João Pessoa (Indian and Afro-Brazilian artefacts); and the Fundação Pierre Chalita in the Palácio do Governo (religious paintings and works by local artists).

THE THREE BEST CARNIVALS OUTSIDE RIO In **Olinda** you can enjoy eleven days of Carnival in the intimacy of a beautifully preserved colonial town. **Salvador**'s famous Carnival involves the whole population, and has an eclectic mix of music. For something different, dance to *carimbó* in **Belém**, boasting a smaller but distinctive Amazonian Carnival.

RIO GRANDE DO NORTE
Natal, The Coast

Natal
The name of the city, meaning "Christmas", commemorates the date of its foundation—December 25, 1599. Located where the Potengi River meets the Atlantic, it is now the state capital, a major port and naval base. Natal juts so far east into the Atlantic that Africa, little more than 3,000 km (1,900 miles) away, is closer than Brazil's own western border. Transatlantic pioneers of aviation took advantage of the geography to fly from Dakar (in Senegal) to Natal. During World War II the US Air Force developed the city's airport as a link between Africa and South America and a base for anti-submarine surveillance.

Forte dos Três Reis Magos
The Portuguese first built a fort to secure the area from hostile Indians and the marauding French. At the tip of the peninsula, the Fort of the Three Wise Men is a star-shaped structure affording splendid views. Construction began on the feast of the Epiphany, January 6, 1598.

Cidade Alta
Despite its 16th-century colonial origins, historic monuments are few and far between in Natal. For a feeling of the colonial era, wander around Praça João Maria, which has an 18th-century cathedral. Slightly older and more distinguished, the church of Santo Antônio is noted for its artfully carved altar and museum of sacred art.

Museu Câmara Cascudo
It covers a wide range of interests from offshore oil production to Indian artefacts and the Afro-Brazilian cult of *umbanda*.

The Coast
South of Natal, Ponte Negra boasts a sweeping bay with calm waters and a sand dune at one end that inclines at 50° into the sea.

Another 10 km (6 miles) south is the splendid Pirangi do Norte, with more fabulous beaches and a cashew tree whose roots are said to cover an astounding 7,300 sq m (8,760 sq yd).

The beaches to the north of Natal, such as Genipabu, are famous for their giant sand dunes. A popular pastime is careering up and down them in beach buggies, which you can hire complete with *bugeiro* (buggy driver). If that sounds too wild a prospect, you can simply hike up the nearest dune and effortlessly toboggan down to sea level.

CEARÁ
Fortaleza, Ceará Coast

Ceará is mainly known for its Costa do Sol—Sunshine Coast—with its 573 km (358 miles) of beaches lapped by the rolling waves of the Atlantic. The lushness of this area contrasts with the *sertão*, the bleak hinterland where the region's cowboys, known as *vaqueiros*, herd cattle and face the danger of drought.

Fortaleza

Capital of Ceará and a significant fishing port, Fortaleza is laid out like a chessboard. Large parks and squares and pastel-coloured or whitewashed buildings inspire a feeling of light and space. It was first settled in 1603 as a base for Pero Coelho de Souza's unsuccessful expeditions into the interior. Fortaleza means "fort" in Portuguese. Conquered by the Dutch in 1637 and recaptured in 1654, the city has long been a place of strategic importance.

The region is renowned for rich and varied arts and crafts traditions—in particular, lacemaking, delicate embroidery, colourful hammocks and naïve painting. It's also one of the world's leading producers of seafood. The shops and restaurants of Fortaleza are more than a match for the pleasures of the seaside.

Centro de Turismo

Practically every visitor to Fortaleza ends up in jail sooner or later. Now known as the Tourist Centre, the old city jail near the seafront, built in 1866, has become the cultural and social heart of the town. Apart from the tourist information office, it also houses an art gallery and a shopping centre for the region's arts and crafts, and the fascinating Museo de Arte e Cultura Populares. The prisoners' exercise yard is now a children's playground.

Mercado Central

Some might prefer the freedom of shopping in the shady labyrinth of the central market on Rua Conde d'Eu, where the stalls overflow with medicinal herbs and essences, fabrics and souvenirs, fish and local produce. Opposite the market, the concrete cathedral in neo-Gothic style is famous for its stained-glass windows.

Teatro José de Alencar

Every Brazilian town has its architectural surprise, and this is Fortaleza's. On a lively market square a few blocks west of the cathedral, the theatre is an example of pure Art Nouveau style, with an abundance of green cast iron and brightly coloured glass, and a practical system of air-conditioning—it has no side walls. The separate cast-iron sections were all brought from Scotland for reassembly here in 1910. The theatre now hosts cultural events.

Museu Histórico e Antropológico do Ceará

East across town, on Avenida Barão de Studart, this museum houses an imposing collection of arms, stamps, paintings and a silver book recording the abolition of slavery in Ceará. The most curious exhibit, though, stands outside—the remains of the light aircraft in which President Castello Branco died near Fortaleza in 1967.

Beaches

If they are not at work, the Fortalezans are out on the sands—especially at Iracema, close to the city near Ponte Metálica, the old port. There is plenty of entertainment here but the water is not recommended for swimming.

There are far better coastal stretches further to the south, in particular the dune-covered Futuro, reached by bus. But if you're looking for something a little quieter, try the northern beaches, Cumbuco and Iparana.

Ceará Coast

At 35 km (22 miles) southeast of Fortaleza, Prainha is the nearest place to sun and swim that seems to escape the city's clutches.

Iguape, 5 km (3 miles) further, is known for the dexterity of its lacemakers. All along this coast you'll see fishermen returning on *jangadas*—low, flat boats with graceful, triangular sails. Try to get a look at the catch—it often includes hammerhead sharks.

Some 240 km (150 miles) northwest of Fortaleza, Jericoacoara is the beach favoured by picture postcards to show off the beauty of Ceará's sea, dunes and palms.

4 THE FOUR BEST BEACHES Brazil has thousands of idyllic strands to choose from, but some stand out. Watch the sunset from on top of the huge sand dunes at **Jericoacoara** in Ceará. Swim in crystal-clear waters at idyllic **Morro de São Paulo**, near Ilhéus. At Florianópolis's **Joaquina** beach, join Brazil's surfing in-crowd. Or pose artfully on Rio's **Copacabana** along with the bold and the beautiful.

MARANHÃO
São Luís, Alcântara

São Luís
The French founded São Luís in 1612 in an attempt to establish an empire in northern Brazil, but they were here a mere three years before being ejected. Their only lasting influence is the city's name, bestowed in honour of Louis XIII. After a later Dutch invasion, the Portuguese concentrated on building up the city.

São Luís was primarily a sugar town. When the industry declined in the 19th century, the colonial buildings declined, too. But things are looking better now: in the 1980s the *Projeto Reviver* saw the restoration of 200 dwellings in the historic city centre.

Historic Centre
Starting at the 18th-century Catedral da Sé, with its fine baroque interior, head a short distance west to the Palácio dos Leões. It began life as a French fort, but the present building dates mainly from the 1760s and is now the state governor's palace.

Wandering south through the main area of the *Projeto Reviver*, look out for the pretty *azulejos* on the façades of the restored colonial mansions. On Rua Jacinto Maia, the Cafua das Mercês is the old slave market, now housing the excellent Museu do Negro. It contains some of the frightening paraphernalia of slave management, such as whips and muzzles, together with an informative exhibition on the history of slavery in the region.

South of here, the 17th-century Igreja do Desterro is in Byzantine style, unusual for Brazil.

Beaches
Ponte d'Areia is only 3.5 km (2 miles) to the north, while Calhau is 7.5 km (over 4 miles). Olho d'Agua and Araçagi, further out, are even nicer. The tide here is famous for the distance it goes out, and the undertow is strong, so be careful when swimming.

Alcântara
Across the Baia de São Marcos, Alcântara is a delightful, crumbling 17th-century colonial town. It used to be the state capital until eclipsed by São Luís. On Praça da Matriz, the *pelourinho*, or whipping-post, was put here in 1647 and bears the arms of the Portuguese Crown. Also on the square, the local museum occupies a restored mansion. Walk along Rua Grande past some handsome colonial houses to church of N.S. do Carmo, dating from the mid-1660s.

The North

Dominated by the mighty Amazon river basin, Brazil's northern region covers half of the country and is made up of seven states: Pará, Amazonas, Acre, Rondônia, Roraima, Amapá and Tocantins. Wilderness wins hands down over civilization; in the whole, vast area there are only two cities of any note, Belém and Manaus. These act as gateways to Amazonia for boat trips along its various rivers and expeditions into the jungle.

AMAZONIA
Belém, Manaus

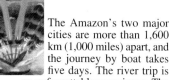

The Amazon's two major cities are more than 1,600 km (1,000 miles) apart, and the journey by boat takes five days. The river trip is an unforgettable experience. The Amazon flows through an area of virgin jungle the size of Europe that is still largely unexplored. Stone Age tribes hunt with blowpipe and poison arrow; jaguars, tapirs and giant anteaters roam the interior. Even for the tourist, cushioned by comfort, travelling the Amazon is an adventure.

The early Portuguese called it O Rio Mar, the River Sea, and its statistics are awesome indeed. From its source in the Andes to its mouth on the Atlantic, the Amazon extends 6,440 km (4,000 miles). Such is its power that the fresh water pumped into the sea spreads out 160 km (100 miles) from the land. Seven of its tributaries—the Japura, Jurua, Madeira, Negro, Purus, Tocantins and Xingu—are each more than 1,600 km (1,000 miles) long. Altogether more than one-sixth of all the world's fresh water is carried in the Amazon system.

Belém
This city of wide boulevards and squares once prided itself on being the Paris of the tropics. Situated near the mouth of the Amazon, it is 120 km (70 miles) from

It brought divas to the jungle: the opulent Teatro Amazonas in Manaus.

the Atlantic. In 1616, the Portuguese built a fort here overlooking Guajara Bay, with the intention of keeping out French, Dutch and English invaders. The settlement took the name N.S. de Belém (Our Lady of Bethlehem) —Belém for short. The town developed because of the sugar trade and produce coming out of the Amazon, but its heyday came with the 19th-century rubber boom. A more recent revival has followed the opening of a road to

HOW THE AMAZON GOT ITS NAME

In 1541, reports came back from Captain Francisco de Orellana's expedition along the great northern river that they had seen tall, fair Indian women leading an attack with bows and arrows. The Portuguese were intrigued by a classical analogy, for the ancient Greeks had believed there existed a race of female warriors living near the Black Sea, whom they called the Amazons. The Brazilian river had been known till then as the Maranon ("That which only God can unravel"). Thenceforth it was called the River of the Amazons, and although subsequent expeditions never sighted any such warlike women, the name stuck.

Brasília in 1960, and the development of mineral projects in the Amazon.

Teatro da Paz

In the centre of the large, pleasant Praça Republica, fringed by mango trees, lush plants and colonial buildings, the theatre comes as quite a surprise. Its rococo pink façade, neoclassical marble columns, and plethora of sculptures and crystal mirrors symbolize the extravagances of the rubber era. The theatre was opened in 1874 after ten years of painstaking planning and construction.

Cidade Velha

West of Praça República, the narrow streets of the old town are packed with shops, venerable buildings and some interesting curiosities. The Igreja das Mercês dates from 1640 and is Belém's oldest church.

Mercado de Ver-o-Paso

A short distance further at the seafront, don't miss the fascinating market. The name, literally "Watch-the-weight", comes from colonial times when Portuguese taxmen would check the weight of products to assess taxes. Go as early as possible to watch the fishermen coming in from the river. Once you've explored the food halls, browse through the more unusual offerings: crocodile-tooth rosaries, bird skeletons, armadillo tails, mysterious herbs and roots to cure—or cause—almost anything.

Forte de Castelo

Just south of the Ver-o-Paso market is the pleasant little harbour, lined with colonial buildings. On the small bluff on the other side, the fort is Belém's "foundation stone", built by the Portuguese in 1616. Climb up to the cannons at the top for a wide-angle view of Guaraja Bay—and a cold drink. This is the most scenic bar in town.

Praça Dom Pedro II

Behind the fort is the stately cathedral, built in 1748, and opposite is Igreja Santo Alexandre, noted for its woodcarving. On nearby Praça Dom Pedro II you will see two archetypal colonial mansions. Palácio Antônio Lemos dates from the 19th century and houses an art museum and the municipal government. Next to it, Palácio Lauro Sodré was once the 18th-century government palace, and now contains the State museum.

Basílica de N.S. de Nazaré

East of the old town on Praça Justo Chermont, this large church was built in 1909 as a replica of St Paul's, Rome. On the second Sunday of October it becomes the focus of one of Brazil's biggest religious festivals, the Círio de Nazaré (Nazareth Candle), a 15-day event that attracts up to half a million people. Downstairs in the basilica, the Museo do Círio documents the event.

Museu Emílio Goeldi

A little further east on Avenida Magalhães Barata, one of the best museums in Brazil covers the

THE FIVE BEST MUSEUMS Brazil's museums cover a vast range of subjects. **Museu Emílio Goeldi** in Belém is part zoo, part museum of the Amazon, part aquarium. Recife's **Museu do Homem do Nordeste** informs about the people and customs of the Northeast. Rio's **Museu da República** in the former presidential palace, celebrates Brazil's life as a Republic since 1889, while the **Museu Nacional** shows off archaeological and ethnographical exhibits from around the country. **Museu de Arte de São Paulo** holds Brazil's finest collection of Western European and Brazilian art.

anthropology, ecology and zoology of the Amazon, summed up best in the pictorial exhibition on the rainforest and the Indians who live there. In the large museum park, an aquarium, zoo and collection of tropical plants give it the air of the jungle. The zoo keeps jaguars, alligators, tapirs, turtles and manatees (large aquatic mammals once taken to be mermaids), allowing you to see Amazonian wildlife that would probably be elusive on any river or jungle trip.

Excursions

The nearest beach, Outeiro, is an hour away by bus and ferry on one of the 2,000 islands spread across the Pará estuary. A dozen other sandy coastal stretches lie in splendid isolation on the Ilha do Mosqueiro. Also across the Pará River (as the Amazon is called here), lies Jaguar Island, a wilderness of equatorial vegetation easily accessible by boat.

Ilha de Marajó

It is definitely worth making the effort to see Marajó, a vast island filling the mouth of the Amazon. It is known as the cradle of the Marajoara civilization, whose descendants still live as they did centuries ago. The island is renowned for its 700,000 water buffalo and thousands of brilliantly coloured tropical birds. You can also see—if you're lucky—sea turtles laying their eggs in the sand. Beaches here are fine for people, too. Allow four hours by boat from Belém port, or 40 minutes by air-taxi.

ETERNAL EL DORADO

Indian tribes had been living in the Amazon for more than 10,000 years before the Spanish discovered it at the beginning of the 16th century. Thereafter, adventurers and traders ventured there, impelled by the lure of gold, cocoa, turtle oil and eventually rubber, in which the region had a monopoly for 40 years.

The Amazon closed itself off to the world again after the end of the rubber boom until the 1970s, when the completion of the Transamazonica Highway opened up the area once more. The Brazilian government encouraged the burning of Amazonia's trees to create farmland for people resettled from other parts of the country, and miners have flooded in to search for gold and iron. It remains to be seen whether the Amazon and its unique environment can survive modern seekers after El Dorado.

Manaus

Like a lost city in the heart of the emerald green wilderness, Manaus lies 1,600 km (1,000 miles) from the sea. Located where the inky black Rio Negro joins the yellow water of the Solimões to form the Amazon, civilization's foothold in the jungle is a patchwork of highrise buildings, pedestrian shopping precincts, modern hotels, old-world mansions and *favelas* (shanty towns) of thatch, wood and tin.

It started as a small outpost of Portuguese colonial trade but burst into the limelight as the centre of the rubber boom. At its peak in the late 19th century, Manaus had electric lighting and trams when most European cities were still under gaslight.

When the golden days ended, the town fell into half a century of decay. But Manaus is once again on the rise. Capital of the vast Amazonas state (Brazil's largest), it stands in a key position at the crossroads of air and river routes and of the network of highways now being slashed through the Amazonian forests.

Manaus is the perfect take-off point for travel to the upper reaches of the Amazon and its many great tributaries, for hunting and fishing expeditions, and for visits to jungle lodges, with the chance to encounter the teeming life of the rainforest.

The Port

On the waterfront, great merchant ships tie up alongside old-fashioned double-decker riverboats and frail covered crafts with outboard motors. Whole families sling their brightly coloured hammocks across the hulls for voyages that might last several days. You will notice that these are floating docks. Built by a British company at the beginning of the 20th century, they serve a vital purpose—the river can rise by up to 30 m (90 ft) in flood season.

In eye-catching Raj style, the Customs House was constructed of imported Scottish stone in 1906. Nearby, the Art Nouveau Mercado Municipal (City Market) sells everything from food and handicrafts to tethered parrots and magic potions.

Teatro Amazonas

Almost as remarkable as the Amazon itself, this elegant Opera House is not to be missed. Every part of the building was imported from Europe over a century ago, when the surrounding Amazon region had scarcely been explored. The structure is Scottish cast iron, the marble came from Italy, the green-blue and gold tiles of the dome from Alsace-Lorraine and the interior furnishings from France. The building was opened in 1896 at the height of the rubber boom. Operatic 73 stars such as Jenny Lind performed here, and Caruso arrived but refused to get off the boat because of a cholera scare. Its very existence here in the jungle has the sort of grandiose craziness about it that inspired Werner Herzog's epic film *Fitzcarraldo*.

Museums

Museu do Homem do Norte, on Avenida 7 de Setembro, examines the anthropology and ecology of the region.

UNLUCKY BOUNCE

The collapse of the rubber market in Brazil at the end of the 19th century can be blamed on an Englishman named Henry Wickham. The Brazilian rubber barons had fought to keep their monopoly of the world's rubber trees. But in 1876, Wickham smuggled out seeds of the precious *Hevea brasiliensis* aboard a steamer, telling the customs officers in Belém that they were rare plants to be presented to Queen Victoria. The seeds were taken to Kew Gardens, cultivated and then re-planted in Britain's colony in Malaya. It proved far more efficient to collect rubber from the orderly Malayan plantations than the wild Amazon, and by 1912 the Brazilian rubber bonanza was finished forever.

Further out, the Museu do Indio at the Salesian Catholic school on Avenida Duque de Caxias, has Indian costumes, weapons, featherwork and other artefacts.

Zoos

The city has two zoos, one in the centre and a much larger selection of animals—established by the army at their jungle training headquarters—further out of the city. Here you will have the chance to see jaguars, tapirs, monkeys, toucans and parrots.

Encontro das Águas

The Meeting of the Waters is a geographical curiosity: 10 km (6 miles) east of Manaus the acid-black waters of the Rio Negro join the clay-yellow Rio Solimões to form the Amazon River. Strangely, the waters do not mix for several kilometres and the river remains black on one side and yellow on the other, before the strains slowly intermingle.

Into the Jungle

Trips can be arranged through operators at any reputable hotel in Manaus. Various companies organize interesting and reliable tours of up to seven days. On all tours outside the city, you would be well advised to join an excursion that has a naturalist attached, who can explain something of the riches of Amazonian life.

Jorge Amado. If there's one writer who has successfully captured the colourful panorama of Brazilian life in print, it's Jorge Amado. Born in Ilhéus in 1912, son of a cocoa planter, Amado has written over 20 novels, which have been translated worldwide. His early titles were influenced by his Marxist beliefs and dealt with the iniquities of the plantation system. However, his most famous works, such as *Gabriela, Clove and Cinnamon* and *Dona Flor and Her Two Husbands*, are big, witty, rollicking books, filled with memorable characters and events, but with an incisive eye on Brazil that makes them thought-provoking as well as fun.

Architecture. Brazil has some of the finest colonial architecture in the Americas. The early Portuguese colonial churches and houses in Salvador and Recife reflect the wealth and confidence of the new colony, based on its sugar plantations. By the 18th century, the gold boom in Minas Gerais was funding the stunning baroque interiors of Ouro Prêto's churches, a match for anything that the old world could create.

During the 19th century, the influence of French architecture held sway. But modern Brazil's sense of daring is unflinching, beholden to no one. São Paulo is perpetually re-inventing itself. The most modern of Latin American cities, it is a metropolis of skyscrapers as far as the eye can see. The work of Oscar Niemeyer, the greatest modern Brazilian architect, can be seen in many Brazilian cities, but the capital, Brasília, contains the largest proportion of his masterpieces. Devotees of architecture of any period will marvel at his modernist cathedral and the concrete arches of the Palácio Itamaraty.

Art and Music. In 1922, after a century of living in the cultural shadow of Europe, Brazilian music, literature and painting were pushed to the forefront. The immediate cause was the celebration of 100 years of independence from Portugal. Brazilian artists rediscovered the importance of Indian and African culture. The samba became a popular theme for composers instead of European dances—Heitor Villa-Lobos's great *Bachianas Brasileiras* is a rewriting of Bach in Brazilian rhythms—and painters such as Cândido Portinari developed techniques and subjects in keeping with contemporary Brazilian life. Today the art galleries, music stores and bookshops are full of exceptional offerings.

Beach Culture. While Rio might not have invented beach culture, it has certainly made it its own. In the 1930s Copacabana became the place for Hollywood stars to be seen, the glamour of its visitors being set off by the natural beauty of the scenery. The Hollywood jet set has moved on, but Rio beach culture is even more vibrant nowadays. The beach is its own world and not simply an adjunct to the city. Indeed, it sometimes seems as if floodlit Copacabana has 24-hour daylight, and you will often find football matches taking place at 3 a.m. During the day, life is free and easy, and beach democracy prevails. You can show off your tan, muscles, sporting prowess or latest jogging outfit if you want to, without feeling an outcast if you possess none of them.

Candomblé. When the Yoruba slaves from Nigeria and Benin were brought to Brazil, their religion came with them. Catholic priests and slave-owners, fearing what they couldn't understand, banned their rituals. The slaves got around this by calling their own gods by Catholic names: Oxala, a god of harvest and procreation, was identified with Jesus; Omolu, the god of healing, was reborn as Lazarus; Ogum, the god of war, became St George.

A candomblé ceremony is a fascinating hybrid of African and Roman religious practice, a church service like no other. Offerings to the gods, made at an altar, are accompanied by drumming, singing and dancing, during which worshippers are ecstatically pos-

sessed by the gods. Many Brazilians today see no problem in practising candomblé alongside Catholicism. Whereas the church hierarchy once thought candomblé would die out, it has proved a remarkably resilient part of Brazil's African heritage.

Carnival. Bigger, brasher and more brilliant than anywhere else, Carnival comes immediately to mind when people think of Brazil. Originally a last bash before Lent, these mega-parties have left religion far behind them. Brazilians throw themselves into the fun with a vengeance, and the samba lasts for days on end. With its sense of spectacle and exuberance, Carnival is the perfect expression of what it means to be Brazilian.

Football. Someone once joked that football isn't a matter of life or death—it's much more important than that. In Brazil you begin to suspect it's the truth. Every citizen is passionately proud of the fact that the national team is the most successful in the world. In 1994 they won the World Cup for a record-breaking fourth time, and some say the resulting national euphoria was a major reason for the government's decision to call a snap election. But more than this, Brazil is recognized everywhere for being a nation of artists in football. Starting with the famous Pelé it has, indeed, made *futebol* the "beautiful game".

77

Shopping

Wherever there's a busy street, square or open patch of land in Brazil, a market is sure to pop up. This is a country devoted to the pursuit of shopping, an activity carried out with the exuberance Brazilians apply to most things in life.

Where to Shop

Towns and cities revel in their enormous shopping malls. In the Conjuncto Nacional in Brasília—a claimant to the title of biggest in South America—and in the ultra-modern Shopping Barra complex in Salvador, you will find high-quality fashion, big department stores and fine food shops in comfortable air-conditioned surroundings. City centres are also crammed with street markets and shops selling everything from the latest electrical goods to ancient herbal remedies.

Duty-Free Articles

If you go to the Amazon, bear in mind that Manaus is a free-trade zone, which means that the price of goods made locally under licence from the multinational companies is lower than in the rest of the country. From the moment you arrive you'll be treated to the sight of crowds of Brazilians staggering under the weight of new TVs, microwave ovens and video recorders.

Antiques

It is worth hunting around for *azulejos*, religious statuettes and other objets from the colonial era.

Arts and Handicrafts

Local artists and craftsmen produce items that make excellent gifts. In Salvador you will see the Bahia doll dressed like the Salvadorean women, in lace, large earrings, and with colourful fruit balanced in a head-basket. These, along with the woodcarvings found in Recife, reflect the African origin of many artisans in the Northeast. Fortaleza is known for its lacework, pottery figurines, artefacts made from bamboo, palm fronds and other natural products, and its highly appealing naïve art, on sale in city and beach markets. In Belém, delightfully intricate wall coverings are available, as well as decorative work made from exotic bird feathers. Further south, in Ouro Prêto, every tourist site will have locals selling soapstone sculptures, the material originating in the nearby quarry.

Shopping opportunities brought right down to the beach.

Indian Arts and Crafts

The government agency responsible for Indian affairs, Fundação Nacional do Indio (FUNAI), runs outlets around the country and at the major airports where Indian artefacts can be bought. Items to look out for include brightly coloured hammocks (essential if you're contemplating a boat trip up the Amazon), woven mats, beads, ceramics and blow-pipes.

Jewellery

Most of the raw material comes from the state of Minas Gerais. Brazil is rich in emeralds, opals, topaz and amethyst, diamonds and rubies. The international dealer H. Stern is found all over the country, but in the big cities such as Rio and Brasília, there are many other jewellers offering cut or uncut stones.

Music and Instruments

From a land where music is as essential to life as food and drink, you can bring back tapes or CDs of samba, bossa nova or folk music. Or why not buy a guitar, a carnivalesque percussion instrument, a flute, or a *berimbau*, an intriguing device of gourd, wood and wire string that in the right hands twangs out the captivating rhythm that accompanies the old slave martial art, *capoeira*.

79

Dining Out

The cuisine is a microcosm of the nation's complex history and geography. The lush farmland of the south produces excellent beef, and the vast river systems of the north guarantee numerous fish recipes. But what happens to these ingredients once they are in the pot is down to the various peoples who have come to Brazil's shores. The Portuguese, Africans in Bahia, Germans in Santa Catarina, Italians and Japanese in São Paulo— have introduced a whole world of styles and traditions.

Breakfast

In all but the humblest hotels, breakfast (*café da manhã*) is a feast of fruit, bread, cheese, ham, coffee and exotic fruit juices.

Lunch

On every Brazilian street at lunchtime, the *lanchonete* is the main focus of attention. These small, unpretentious restaurants serve enormous portions of decent, down-to-earth food. Very popular now are the self-service, or *por kilo*, versions. Pick up a plate and go to the counter, and heap on whatever takes your fancy from its several hot trays of chicken, meat, beans, rice, vegetables, and so on. At the other end someone weighs your plate and you pay in relation to the price per kilo. It's an enjoyable, and inexpensive, alternative to the restrictions of the set menu.

The National Dish

Without a doubt, *feijoada* can claim to unify the country, at least at the culinary level. There are regional variations, but the recurring theme is a tasty concoction of black beans with sausage, pork and smoked meat, flavoured with onions, garlic, coriander, tomato, parsley and perhaps hot peppers. An accompanying soup plate is filled with boiled white rice (*arroz*), over which the *feijoada* is spooned. Sprinkled with manioc flour and garnished with shredded kale, spring greens and fresh orange slices, it's a meal to fortify you for even the hardest day at the beach.

Fish and Seafood

Fish (*peixe*) is a mainstay of the diet, particularly in the North and Northeast. *Filet de peixe* is a standard fish fillet, usually bass. Also

Tropical fruit ripe for the picking at a roadside stall.

try *linguado* (sole) and *dourado*, a tasty freshwater fish. The Brazilians have spiced up Portugal's fish chowders, notably *caldeirada* or *frutos do mar ensopados*, as well as *bacalhau* (dried salt cod) baked in a rich sauce.

In Recife, most menus feature steamed fish fillet with a thick shrimp sauce, while on the north coast *peixe a delícia* is, as the name suggests, a delicious fish dish cooked in banana and coconut milk.

Fortaleza is one of the world's leading producers of spiny lobster, and it tastes even better if eaten fresh at a restaurant on Futuro beach.

Meat

You'll end up eating a lot of meat in Brazil, especially if you stay in the south. Not to be missed is the popular *churrasco*, which has increasingly spread nationwide. Be prepared to confront huge quantities of the most succulent barbecued beef, chicken and whatever else finds its way onto the skewer. Originating as a gaucho meal eaten on the hoof in Rio Grande do Sul, nowadays it is served at restaurants known as *churrascarias*. Many of them have a fixed price *(rodízio)* for as much as you can eat, so make sure you've an extra notch to let out on your belt before you go.

In standard restaurants, asking for *bife* or *file* will get you a steak, and *frango* or *galinha*, chicken. An interesting choice is *xinxim de galinha*, a chicken stew cooked with dried shrimp and a fiery side-sauce.

Bahian Cuisine

The state of Bahia was once the centre of colonial Brazil and received the majority of West African slaves to work on its sugar and coffee plantations. Some were allowed to fish for shrimps and clams, and these local ingredients were cooked in methods remembered from African homelands. Bahian food is the result. It is flavoursome, spicy and ruled by the strong taste of the *dendê* (palm oil) in which it is usually cooked.

Vatapá is a purée of shrimp and ground fish, usually grouper, cooked with dendê oil, coconut milk, pieces of bread, coriander, tomato, ginger, garlic, peppers and cashew nuts, and served with rice. *Carurú* again uses shrimp and grouper, but is accompanied by a tangy sauce made from okra and red peppers. *Moqueca* is seafood cooked in a clay pot, with a powerful coconut and dendê oil flavour and spiced up by a hot pepper sauce. Not for the fainthearted, *sarapatel* is sheep or pig's liver stewed with onions, peppers, tomatoes and the animal's fresh blood. Finally, *acarajé* is a snack sold by street vendors; it consists of a batter of dried beans and dried shrimp, deep-fried in—what else?—boiling dendê oil.

Cuisine of the Amazon

Unsurprisingly, for a vast region that was until recently inaccessible to the rest of Brazil, Amazonia has a notable cuisine of its own, derived from the river which dominates the area, and the Indians who once nurtured it. A traditional Indian ingredient is manioc. You will soon become familiar with the pungent taste of this root, for it appears everywhere and in various guises—fried, boiled, and powdered.

The river fish is excellent, especially *tambaqui*, *tucanare* and the succulent *pirarucu*. Don't expect a whole one—they grow as big as a basketball player. A memorable delicacy is *pato no tucupi*, duck served in a tingling aromatic sauce made from manioc juice mixed with peppers. *Tacacá* is an Indian soup prepared with dried shrimp, garlic, manioc and *jambu*, a local herb. *Maniçoba* is a dish best eaten at a good restaurant; some of the ingredients can take up to a week to prepare. They include *maniva* (manioc leaf), *mocotó* (beef marrow), *jába* (sun-dried meat), ham and sausage.

Other Cuisines

If, after sampling all the indigenous wonders, you still have room for more, there are a few surprises left to you. In pronouncedly German towns such as Blumenau and Joinville, you can eat schnitzels as good as any on the Rhine. The Italian food in Rio and São Paulo is first-rate, and the many Japanese restaurants in the Liberdade area of São Paulo are uniformly excellent.

Desserts

In Bahia try *quindim*, a vanilla-flavoured coconut cake, sometimes stuffed with prunes or fried bananas, and sprinkled with icing sugar. Nothing, however, beats the amazing array of tropical fruits on offer—more than a hundred succulent varieties—fresh or as a sorbet or ice cream.

Drinks

Brazil's most popular aperitif, the *caipirinha*, is a cocktail based on *cachaça*, a throat-scouring spirit distilled from sugar-cane and also known as *aguardente*, or "burning water". One sip and you'll know why. Take care if you decide to drink it neat. With lime, sugar and ice added, it's very enjoyable.

Brazilian wines from the far south come in red, white and rosé, and although they have still to reach the quality of Chilean and Argentinian vintages, they are nevertheless a pleasant accompaniment to local cuisine. Brazilian beer, on the other hand, is always extremely good. The cold draft beer, *chopp* (pronounced "shoppee"), is refreshing, while bottled beers such as Antarctica, Brahma and Kaiser slip down very easily.

Guaraná is a popular soft drink made from the berries of an Amazonian shrub and supposed to be good for you. *Sucos*, fruit juices, are works of art. They come in a variety of extraordinary flavours, passion fruit *(maracujá)*, including papaya *(mamão),* cashew *(cajú)* and guava *(goiaba)*. But then there are juices from fruits which have no translation—*acerola*, the dark, bitter *açaí*, tangy *cupuaçú*, *graviola* and *tapereba*. Juices are often served with sugar and ice, but ask for them *natural* or *sem açúcar* if you don't want any extras. Bear in mind, though, that some of these unfamiliar fruits are very bitter indeed.

Coffee

Finally, after lunch or dinner, many restaurants offer a complimentary coffee—it is, after all, a Brazilian's birthright. They like it very sweet, very strong and very often. While you're about it, buy a few packages to take home. Whatever your taste, there's bound to be a blend just for you.

Sports

It might seem at times that everyone in Brazil is out jogging, speed-walking or playing football. With great year-round weather and over 7,000 km (4,350 miles) of coastline, it's not hard to see why it's an outdoor country for all to enjoy.

Water Sports

There's no shortage of inviting places to swim in Brazil. The northeast coast in particular has miles of deserted coastline away from industrial areas, the main problem for healthy swimming around the big cities.

Surfing is very popular, and the waves are especially good in the south. Florianópolis is host to the Brazilian championships, and any bus heading to the beach seems to have its share of surfers on board. The best time for surfing is in winter (July to September).

Windsurfing takes place all around the Brazilian coast, and you should ask at the Tourist Office about where to hire equipment.

In the Clouds

Brazil provides some exciting climbing. Sugar Loaf mountain, with over 30 routes, must surely offer the world's greatest urban climb, but there are challenges to be had throughout Brazil's national and state parks.

If you want to risk life and limb and enjoy the view at the same time, then you can always try hang-gliding, a sport particularly in vogue around Rio.

Hiking

Best undertaken in the winter months, hiking in the national and state parks is a rewarding experience. Check out the Parque Nacional da Chapada Diamantina in Bahia, follow the old pioneer trails in the Marumbi State Park near Curitiba, or Tijuca in Rio.

Spectator Sports

The national game is *futebol*. No visit would be complete without seeing a game at the Maracaná stadium in Rio, a cauldron of passion with a capacity of 150,000.

The Brazilian Grand Prix is one of the major international Formula One race meetings. Brazil has had considerable success in this sport, with champions such as Emerson Fittipaldi and Nelson Piquet keeping it at the forefront of public interest.

The Hard Facts

Airports

Several airlines, including three Brazilian carriers—Varig, VASP and Transbrasil—have regular direct flights from Europe to Rio de Janeiro and São Paulo, and to a lesser extent, Recife on the northeast coast. From the United States, flights also go from Miami to Manaus and Belém, both in the north of the country, and to the capital Brasília.

In Rio, international flights land at Galeão Airport, 15 km (9 miles) north of the city. There is a good air-conditioned executive bus service, Empresa Real, which whisks you off to the city centre and the beaches at Copacabana, Ipanema, etc. Taxis are plentiful but not a cheap option. São Paulo's international airport, Aeroporto de Cumbica, is 30 km (19 miles) east of the city and buses go from there to the Praça da República in the city centre.

Airports are well equipped with bank and change facilities, car-hire firms, hotel-booking desks, shops, post offices, restaurants, etc.

Prior to each internal flight you will have to pay an airport tax, payable in *reais,* and when you leave Brazil there will be a departure tax payable in US dollars.

Climate

As 92 per cent of Brazil is situated in the southern hemisphere, summer is from December to February, and winter from July to September. In summer, Brazil seems uniformly hot, and the climate unrelentingly tropical. There are some seasonal and regional variations, however. Winter temperatures in São Paulo can reach as low as 10°C (50°F), and it even snows occasionally in the southernmost states. Rio can hit a scorching 38°C (100°F) with high humidity in January. It is always humid in the Amazon, with sporadic, torrential rainfall from December to May. Having said that, you will rarely need more than light clothing in Brazil, and although the intensity of rain throughout the country can amaze, it never lasts for long and can easily and pleasurably be avoided by ducking into a bar or café for half an hour.

Communications

Post offices *(correios)* are open Monday to Friday from 9 a.m. to 5 p.m., and Saturday from 9 a.m. to 1 p.m. Apart from handling mail and providing international telephone services, the larger offices will send and receive faxes, telexes and telegrams for you. The cost of postage is relatively high.

Public call boxes are immediately recognizable. Their large shells appear in various colours and are known affectionately in Brazil as *orelhões*, or big ears. You will find two types of phone. The older red ones take *fichas*, tokens obtainable from newsstands or special streetside token-sellers. These are usually for local calls only. It is far more convenient to buy phonecards *(cartãos telefônicas)*, which are for use in the newer, black telephones. Newsstands sell mainly the 20-unit cards, although you can also find them for 35 and 70 units. You can make interstate (and sometimes international) calls from these telephones.

To phone abroad from Brazil, dial 00 (international code) followed by the country code (1 for USA and Canada, 44 for UK) the area code (minus the initial zero) and the number. To call Brazil from overseas, dial the international access code + 55 + city code (minus the initial zero) + number. The city code for Rio is 021, São Paulo 011, Brasília 061, Recife 081, Salvador 071.

Consulates

Embassies are situated in the capital, Brasília, and many countries also have consulates in São Paulo and Rio de Janeiro, as well as other cities around Brazil.

Telephone numbers for foreign embassies in Brasília:

Britain (061) 225 2710
USA (061) 321 7272
Canada (061) 321 2171

Telephone numbers for Brazilian embassies abroad:

Britain (020) 7499 0877
USA (212) 757-3080
Canada (613) 237-1090

Crime

There is undoubtedly a wild side to Brazil, and it has not always enjoyed a reputation for safety. But the Brazilian government takes the issue very seriously and you will often find the major tourist areas have at least one policeman on every corner. Moreover, these dangers only really apply to the bigger cities, and if you follow a few basic precautions, you will be as secure as in any other major urban area. Leave valuables in the hotel safe *(cofre)*, don't carry large sums of money or wear expensive jewellery, wristwatches, etc., and keep cameras and handbags securely fastened and as inconspicuous as possible. Keep away from isolated parts of the city, especially at night. A concealed moneybelt is useful, but keep a supply of small change in your pocket so that you don't have to fiddle with it in public.

87

Customs

Each tourist may import 2 litres of wine or spirits, in addition to any goods with a total value not exceeding 500 US$ or equivalent. You may also import articles purchased at the duty-free shops of Brazilian airports, up to a value of 500 US$ or equivalent.

Driving

To rent a car you will need a credit card, valid driver's licence and passport. Most of the hire firms charge similar prices, which are fairly expensive, but if you are sharing and want to get to out-of-the-way beaches, it might be a good way to do it. Unfortunately, Brazilian roads leave much to be desired, and the drivers even more—the country is usually near the top of the road fatalities league, averaging around 30,000 deaths a year, 20 per cent of the world total.

Many cars run on *alcool*, a mixture of petrol and ethanol extracted from sugarcane, so check before you drive off. Fuel prices are closer to the European than US level. Don't count on filling stations accepting credit cards, especially outside the big cities: make sure you have enough cash.

Electric Current

Currents vary throughout the country—in Rio de Janeiro the supply is 110 or 120 volts, 60 cycles AC, with 220-volt outlets in large hotels. In São Paulo it's 110 volts. Recife and Brasília have a 220-volt service, and Salvador uses 127-volt outlets! Take an adaptor and always check prior to use.

Emergencies

There is no single nationwide emergency number to call. Check at your hotel reception in each city. Alternatively, public phones are marked with the numbers for fire *(bombeiros)* and police *(polícia civil)*.

Formalities

Visitors from most EC countries need only a valid passport to enter Brazil. Those from the United States, Canada and Australia must obtain visas prior to departure. On the way to Brazil you will need to fill in an entry card. The carbon copy is given back to you and should be kept until you leave the country, as it may cause problems—and even a fine—if you cannot produce it.

Health

For peace of mind it is essential to take out health insurance before going to Brazil. The most dangerous thing you face, however, may just be the power of the sun. A good sunblock, a hat, and avoiding long midday sunbathing are the best precautions.

It is wise to drink plenty of mineral water (never tap water), and be wary of salads and unpeeled fruit. Brazilian cities have pharmacies (*farmácias*) on virtually every street, so you can always obtain the basic medicines and drugs.

While the threat of malaria, cholera and yellow fever is fairly low along the coast, there are several exotic diseases lurking inland, particularly in the Amazon region. If you are going there, start a course of malaria tablets at least a week before departure. Yellow fever inoculations are not compulsory in order to enter Amazonia, but consult the Brazilian Embassy, as well as your doctor or airport health centre, to find out what precautions you should take before leaving. Malaria and yellow fever are both carried by mosquitoes, so don't forget to bring a good insect repellent.

Holidays and Festivals

Shops and offices are closed on the following national holidays:

January 1	*New Year's Day*
April 21	*Tiradentes Day*
May 1	*Labour Day*
September 7	*Independence Day*
October 12	*Our Lady of Aparecida Day*
November 2	*All Souls' Day*
November 15	*Proclamation of Republic*
December 25	*Christmas Day*

Moveable holidays:

May or June	*Corpus Christi*
March or April	*Good Friday and Easter*

Moveable festival: *Carnival*

In addition, there are various additional state holidays. Inquire at your hotel.

Language

The national and official language of Brazil is Portuguese. There are approximately 170 different indigenous languages spoken by around 300,000 Indians. Staff at the larger hotels and tourist offices in the big cities speak some English and French. German is spoken widely in towns in Santa Catarina. Spanish speakers may be able to cope in Portuguese with some concentration and effort, although the Brazilian accent may take some getting used to.

A little Portuguese goes a long way with Brazilians, and accompanied by the internationally recognized thumbs-up sign, you will be surprised how easy it is to get your point across.

Media

If you don't read Portuguese, the news may pass you by for the duration of your stay in Brazil. European newspapers slowly filter through to the main tourist parts of Rio and São Paulo. American papers such as the *Miami*

Herald and the *International Herald Tribune* are more widely available.

At most medium-priced and expensive hotels you should find CNN on cable TV. In the south of the country the large German community ensures a number of German channels on hotel cable television. The incurable news addict should consider taking along a shortwave radio and a list of local wavelengths from the BBC World Service.

Money

The unit of currency is the *real* (R$ or BRL), plural: *reais*, which is divided into 100 *centavos* (c). Coins are issued in denominations of 1, 5, 10, 25, 50 *centavos* and 1 *real*; banknotes 1, 5, 10, 50 and 100 *reais*. The coins are very similar so check them carefully when you receive change.

Since the introduction of the *real* in 1994, the Brazilian currency has been tied to the American dollar. The dollar is worth slightly more at present, but US banknotes are accepted throughout the country usually at par with the *real*. As the *real* cannot be bought outside Brazil, it's a good idea to take some US dollars in cash and some in traveller's cheques. In recent years, Brazilian banks' ATMs have been linked to the world banking system, and if you have a cash-card with the Visa facility, for example, it can be used at 24-hour-a-day cash machines of the Bradesco Bank. This is possibly the safest way to obtain local currency. Finally, many hotels and restaurants welcome credit cards.

Opening Hours

The following times are intended as a general guide and will often be subject to local variations.

Banks open Monday to Friday 10 a.m.–4 or 4.30 p.m.

Offices usually open 9 a.m.–6 p.m.

Shops are open Monday to Friday 9 a.m.–6.30 or 7 p.m., and Saturdays 9 a.m.–1 p.m. Shopping centres may stay open until 10 p.m. Apart from tourist shops and restaurants, very few are open on Sunday.

Hours for *museums* vary considerably, so be sure to check with your hotel reception or the local tourist office. Most museums are shut all day Monday.

Religion

Although the republican constitution of 1889 deprived Brazil of a state religion, it is the largest Catholic nation on earth, with nearly 90 per cent of the population adhering to the Church of Rome. There are increasing numbers of Protestants, testament to the influence of American missionaries, as well as a small percentage of Jews, Muslims and Buddhists, the latter a reflection of Brazil's Japanese population. Candomblé, a cult brought by slaves from West Africa, still has a substantial following, particularly in the Northeast.

Time Zones

Brazil spreads over four time zones. The eastern islands of Fernando de Noronha keep to GMT–2. The eastern segment of the mainland, including Salvador, Rio and Brasília, is GMT–3. West of this, at a longitude which goes through the Amazonian city Manaus, it is GMT–4. In the far west of Amazonia and the small state of Acre bordering on Peru, the clocks are set at GMT–5.

Tipping

At most restaurants, a 10 per cent *taxa de serviço* will be added to the bill. But given that the wages are quite low, you may wish to top that up if the service has been good. There's no need to tip taxi drivers, but it may seem churlish not to round off the fare. It is customary to tip hotel employees such as maids, and porters at airports, etc.

Toilets

Public toilets can be off-putting (airports and Rodoviária are honourable exceptions), so you might prefer to make use of the facilities in a café or bar. It is only polite to order a drink if you do so. Toilets are signposted as *Banheiro* or *Sanitario*. The men's are marked *Cavalheiros* or *Masculinos,* the women's *Senhoras* or *Damas.*

Tourist Information

The Brazilian Tourist Board, Embratur, has its headquarters in Brasília and an office in Rio de Janeiro. For addresses, see inside back cover. Elsewhere, tourist offices are sponsored by individual states and cities.

Transport

Air

The only way to get around with any speed is by plane. Consequently, almost every Brazilian city is equipped with a sizable, modern airport. These generally have car-hire firms, hotel-booking desks and bank cashpoint facilities in the arrivals area.

Local buses take you to the centre, although this can be a very slow process indeed. Taxis often charge increased tariffs to and from airports. You may wish to pre-pay with a taxi ticket purchased at the ticket office *(bilheteria).*

Air travel in Brazil is very expensive. An Airpass is obtainable from the three Brazilian national carriers, Varig, VASP and Transbrasil, who all offer similar deals. You must buy a minimum of five 91 flights, with the possibility of going up to a maximum of nine. Travel must be completed within three weeks and the airpass can only be bought outside Brazil. If you're thinking of heading off to more remote parts of the country, remember that one flight bought locally can cost nearly as much as an entire Airpass.

Inter-urban buses

If you have plenty of time and wish to see the countryside, then the buses are an economical option. Modern, clean and usually with a toilet on board, they criss-cross Brazil and reach just about every corner of the country. The drivers are exceptions to the generally deplorable Brazilian road skills (and buses are restricted to 80 km per hour), and the buses leave promptly. Many routes have *executivo*, or air-conditioned buses, available at a higher price. For approximately double the ordinary price you can catch an overnight *leito*, with three reclining seats to a row and equipped with blankets, pillows, a coffee machine and mineral water. You miss the scenery, of course, but save on hotel bills. They make regular stops en route, and you'll find the Brazilian service stations are pleasantly clean and with good canteens.

Buses leave from the *Rodoviária* (bus station), handier to the town centres than the airports. In Rio, Empresa Real runs an *executivo* bus to the centre and the beaches. In São Paulo, Recife and Porto Alegre, the bus stations are connected to the centre by efficient metro systems.

Local buses

These are nowhere as sleek as their inter-urban cousins. In Rio, you get on at the back and pay the conductor before passing through a turnstile. Hold on tight because the driver is apt to take off like Nelson Piquet. In Brasília and São Paulo, you have to get on at the front.

The local buses are an excellent way of getting around most Brazilian cities, much cheaper than taxis and allowing you to mingle with the locals. They tend to get pretty crowded, so when it approaches your stop, make sure you've worked your way to the front of the bus.

Trains

There are very few public train services. You can go from São Paulo to Santos, Rio or Brasília, but the best trip is undoubtedly the famous Curitiba to Paranaguá train.

Metro

Rio, São Paulo and Recife have excellent metro systems that are inexpensive, safe and frequent.

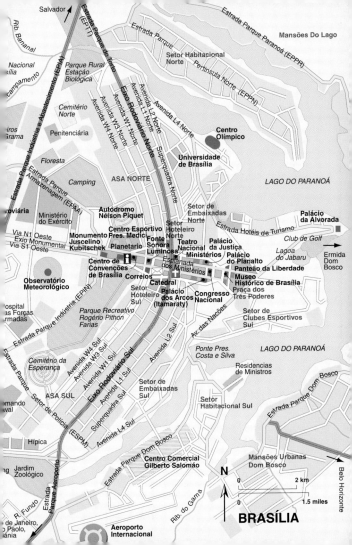

BRASÍLIA

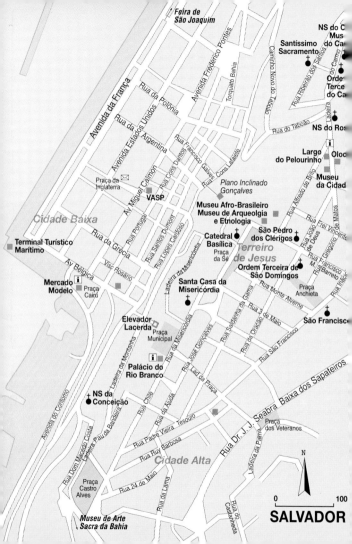

Feira de
São Joaquim

NS do C
Mus
do Ca

Santíssimo
Sacramento

Orde
Terce
do Ca

NS do Ros

Largo
do Pelourinho

Oloc

Museu
da Cidade

Plano Inclinado
Gonçalves

Museu Afro-Brasileiro
Museu de Arqueolgia
e Etnologia

Catedral
Basílica

São Pedro
dos Clérigos

Cidade Baixa

Praça da
Inglaterra

VASP

Terminal Turístico
Marítimo

Terreiro
de Jesus

Praça
da Sé

Ordem Terceira de
São Domingos

Santa Casa da
Misericórdia

Praça
Anchieta

Mercado
Modelo

Praça
Cairú

São Francisco

Elevador
Lacerda

Praça
Municipal

Palácio do
Rio Branco

NS da
Conceição

Praça
dos Veteranos

Cidade Alta

Praça Castro
Alves

Museu de Arte
Sacra da Bahia

0   100

N

SALVADOR

Avenida da França
Rua da Polônia
Rua dos Estados Unidos
Avenida Estados Argentina
Rua Cons Dantas
Rua Francisco Galvea
Rua Cons Lafaiê
Avenida Frederico Pontes
Torquato Bahia
Caminho Novo do Taboão
Rua Ribeirão dos Santos
Rua do Carmo
Ladeira do Carmo
Rua do Taboão
Ladeira
Av Miguel Calmon
Rua Portugal
Rua Santos Dumont
Rua Lopes Cardoso
Rua da Grécia
Visc Rosário
Av Bélgica
Ladeira da Misericórdia
Rua Alfredo de Brito
Rua Frei Vincente
Rua Greg?rio de Matos
Rua Francisco M
Rua Barreto
Rua Inácio
Rua de Deus
Rua Monte Alverne
Rua Saldanha da Gama
Rua 3 de Maio
Rua da Misericórdia
Rua João Gonçalves
Rua do Orat?rio
Rua São Francisco
Lad da Praça
Rua Chile
Rua da Ajuda
Rua Padre Vieira
Tesouro
Rua Ruy Barbosa
Rua Dr. J. J. Seabra
Baixa dos Sapateiros
Ladeira de Montanha
Ladeira de Pamã
Rua 24 de Maio
Rua da Lama
Rua Dom Macedo Costa
Ladeira Pau da Bandeira
Avenida do Contorno
Rua do Cabeçaneda

Rio Anil

Ponte
José Samey

Igreja dos Remedios

Rua Jonsem Miller

Avenida Beira Mar

Rua do Machado

Rua 15 de Novembro

Rua da Ribeirão

Rua da Savedro

Rua Riacho

Rua
Graça Aranha

Beco dos Barqueiros

Rua do Egito

Rua
Santo Antônio

Praça
Antônio
Lobo

Santo Antônio

Palácio
dos Leões

Rua da Silva

Sé

Rua do Alecrim

Praça D. Pedro II.

Sebrae

**Fonte do
Riberão**

Maratur

Rua das Afogados

Rua de Nazaré

VASP

**Museu Histórico do
Estado de Maranhão**

**Museu de
Arte Visuais**

**Mercado
Praia Grande**

Rua do Sol

Rua do Cruz

Rua dos Cravelros

Rua Portugal

Rua São João

São João

oviária

**Centro do
Criatividade**

Rua Humberto
de Campos

Carmo

Rua da Paz

Rua do Comercio

Rua da Alfândega

Praça
João
Lisboa

Trav. da
Passagem

Rua Flores

Museu de Arte Sacre

Rua João Vital

Rua da Palma

Rua Grande

Tr. Boaventura

Rua da Estrela

Godofredo Viana

Beco da Prensa

Avenida Magalhães de Almeida

Rua de Santana

Projeto

Rua 28 de Julho

Rua Afonso Pena

Beco Escuro

Rua de São Pantaleão

Reviver

Rua Direita

Rua
Regente Braulio

Rua do Deserto

Rua do Saúde

Rua do Mocambo

Avenida Senador Vitorino Feira

**Cafua das Mercês
Museu do Negro**

**Fonte das
Pedras**

Rua do Inveja

Rua Jacinto Maia

Rua de Manga

Praça do Mercado

Rua Luciano Reis

**Convento
das Mercês**

Portinho

**Mercado
Central**

Igreja de São Pantaleão

Travessa da Lapa

T. do
M. Central

Rua de Pelho

T. do
Gasometro

Rua Antônio Rayol

Rua
Candido

Rua da Cotovia

**San José
do Desterro**

Avenida Guaxenduba

Ribeira

Rua das Cajazeiras

Tr. Fonte do Bisp

Rua do Santiago

N

250

Rua Ivar
Saldanha

SÃO LUÍS

Centro de Artesanato

INDEX

Alcântara 67
Aleijadinho 31
Amado, Jorge 76
Amazonia 69–74
Angra dos Reis 21
Aparados da Serra 42
Architecture 76
Bahia 53–58
Belém 68–72
Belo Horizonte 29–30
Blumenau 39–40
Boa Viagem 60
Brasília 43–49
Campo Grande 51
Candomblé 77
Capoeira 55
Carnival 62, 77
Ceará 64–65
Chapada dos
   Guimarães 50
Ciudad del Este 38
Copacabana 18
Corcovado 20
Cuiabá 50
Curitiba 35–36
Domingos Martins 27
Encontro das Águas 74
Espírito Santo 32
Florianópolis 39
Football 77
Fortaleza 64–65
Igaraçu 62
Iguaçu Falls 37–38
Ilhabela 26
Ilhéus 56–58
Ipanema 18
Itaipú Dam 38
Itamarcá 62
Joinville 40
Jungle trips 74
Maceio 62
Manaus 73–74
Maracaná 20

Marajó, Ilha de 72
Maranhão 67
Mato Grosso 50–51
Mato Grosso do Sul 51
Minas Gerais 29–31
Natal 63
Niemeyer, Oscar
   49, 76
Niterói 21
Olinda 60–62
Ouro Prêto 30–31
Pantanal 50–51
Paraná 35–38
Paranaguá 36–37
Parati 21
Pelotas 42
Pernambuco 59–62
Petrópolis 21
Porto Alegre 41–42
Porto Seguro 58
Recife 59–60
Rio de Janeiro 13–20
Rio Grande 42
Rio Grande do Norte 63
Rio Grande do Sul
   42–43
Salvador da Bahia
   53–56
Santa Catarina 39–40
Santa Catarina,
   Ilha de 39
Santos 26
São Francisco
   do Sul 40
São José do Norte 43
São Luis 67
São Paulo 22–25
Sugar Loaf 17–18
Tijuca National Park 19
Trains 36, 51
Vila Velha State Park
   37
Vitória 27

GENERAL EDITOR:
   Barbara Ender-Jones
EDITOR:
   Mark Little
LAYOUT:
   Luc Malherbe
PHOTO CREDITS:
   Mireille Vautier front cover,
      pp.5, 7, 10, 28, 47, 48, 61, 66
      69, 75, 81, 85 (background)
   Hémisphères:
      Frances back cover, pp. 12,
      19, 44–45, 53, 57
   Giraudou pp. 32–33, 79,
      85 (bottom)
   Lescourret p. 16
   Guignard p. 34
MAPS:
   Elsner & Schichor
   Huber Kartographie
   JPM Publications

Copyright © 2000
by JPM Publications S.A.
12, avenue William-Fraisse,
1006 Lausanne, Switzerland
E-mail:
information@jpmguides.com
Web site:
http://www.jpmguides.com/

Printed in Switzerland
Gessler/Sion (CTF)

Rua Paula Souza

IFIGÉNIA

Queiroz

Rua Carlos de Souza

Rua da Cantareira

Avenida do Estado

Mendes Caldeira

N

0   300 m

SÃO PAULO

Avenida Mercúrio

Mercado
Municipal

Rua da 25 de Março

Av. P. Mata

Viaduto
Diário Popular

Rua da Assunção

BRAS

Rua do Gasómetro

Aeroporto Internacional

Parque
Dom Pedro II

Av do Estado

Avenida Rangel Pestana

Avenida Exterior

Rua Gen Carneiro

Rua 25 de Março

Avenida Rangel Pestana

Patio
do Colégio

Museu Padre
Anchieta

Solar de
Marquesa
de Santos

Pedro II
M

Boa Vista

Igreja da Terc.
Ordem do Carmo

Rua do Carmo

Rua Carmelitas

Sé
M

Garibaldi

Praça
da Sé

Rua S. Martins

Rua Visconde de Pamaíba

Catedral
Metropolitana

Rua Tabatinguera

Av Alcântara Machado

Rua Amaral

Rua Cons Furtado

Rua Conde de Sarzedos

Costa E Silva

Rua dos Estudantes

Avenida do Estado

Santos